TRUE CRIMES
OF THE BIBLE

SCANDAL.
MURDER.
ADULTERY.
FORGIVENESS.
FAITH.
HOPE.

DR. BRUCE BECKER

Published by Straight Talk Books
P.O. Box 301, Milwaukee, WI 53201
800.661.3311 • timeofgrace.org

Copyright © 2023 Time of Grace Ministry

All rights reserved. This publication may not be copied, photocopied, reproduced, translated, or converted to any electronic or machine-readable form in whole or in part, except for brief quotations, without prior written approval from Time of Grace Ministry.

Scripture is taken from THE HOLY BIBLE, NEW INTERNATIONAL VERSION®, NIV®. Copyright © 1973, 1978, 1984, 2011 by Biblica, Inc.® Used by permission. All rights reserved worldwide.

Printed in the United States of America
ISBN: 978-1-949488-74-6

TIME OF GRACE *is a registered mark of Time of Grace Ministry.*

CONTENTS

Introduction 5
Cain 7
Moses 16
King David 26
King David's Family 40
Ehud 53
Jael 63
The Levite and His Concubine 72
Ahab and Jezebel 86
The Herods 98
Paul 112
Conclusion 125

INTRODUCTION

I think I know what you're thinking. You're thinking, *"What do the crimes recorded in the Bible, crimes that were committed thousands of years ago, have to do with me?"* Now even if you weren't thinking this, it's a valid question. Let me try to answer it.

Let's start with something the wisest man in the world said three thousand years ago. King Solomon wrote, **"What has been will be again, what has been done will be done again; there is nothing new under the sun"** (Ecclesiastes 1:9). Crimes that impact our society today are no different than those committed thousands of years ago. There's nothing new under the sun.

However, what makes the criminals and crimes in the Bible significant for us goes beyond an ancient police report that details the crime. With each of the crimes we will investigate in this book, we'll also delve into God's response to each crime as we learn from the Bible. (Spoiler alert! God doesn't respond to each crime the same way.) It is in God's response that we find lessons to be learned for us Christians living today.

In this book, we'll take a look at ten crimes in the Bible. Some will be familiar to you, others maybe not. For each crime, we'll investigate who committed it, how God responded to the criminal, and what we can learn from it. By the end of this book (and quite possibly before!), I pray you will be amazed by God's holiness, justice, mercy, and love.

In the spirit of being upfront and transparent, this book didn't start out as a book. It actually started out as a podcast series from my podcast, *Bible Threads With Dr. Bruce Becker*.

The idea for the series came from two sources. One was from a previous visit to my family in Washington State. During the evenings that my wife and I were there, the adults in the room watched a TV series on Hulu called *Only Murders in the Building*. It's a comedy series that stars Steve Martin, Martin Short, and Selena Gomez. That got me thinking along the lines of . . . *Only Murders in the Bible*.

The other input for the series came from some of my colleagues at Time of Grace. In discussing the idea with them, they suggested I should investigate true crimes in the Bible. So that's how *True Crimes: Bible Edition* was born. It's been a popular podcast, so the Time of Grace team decided we should put it into print for those who prefer to read books instead of listening to podcasts.

You're holding the result. Let's get started with *True Crimes of the Bible*.

CAIN

There's no better place to start than with the first crime recorded in the Bible. It was committed by the son of the first couple, Adam and Eve, whom God had created in his own image. That image of God was compromised when Satan perpetrated what is actually the most disastrous deception in the universe and in all the world's history. It's when Satan tempted Adam and Eve to disobey God's one rule of not eating from the tree of the knowledge of good and evil. One of the consequences of their disobedience was that, throughout history, serious crimes would be committed by people against people. The first crime recorded in the Bible is the crime of murder committed by Adam and Eve's son Cain against his younger brother Abel.

Genesis chapter 4 begins: **"Adam made love to his wife Eve, and she became pregnant and gave birth to Cain"** (verse 1). Later, as Eve held baby Cain in her arms, she expressed these words: **"With the help of the LORD I have brought forth a man"** (Genesis 4:1). In the original Hebrew, the word order is inverted and literally reads, "I have brought forth a man with the help of the LORD." Some Bible scholars, including the reformer

Martin Luther, translated this as, "I have brought forth a man, the Lord." Such a translation suggested that Eve thought her son was the Lord, the One who would crush the head of the serpent. But that's not what the Hebrew text says. There is a preposition in front of the word "Lord" that means "with" or "with the help of." So the better translation is, "I have brought forth a man with the help of the Lord."

There are two other things worth noting in this single statement of Eve. When Eve testified that the birth of her son was done with the Lord's help, she was acknowledging that God had allowed her to participate in his creation of a new human life. It's a testimony to the miracle of every newborn baby. Second, when Eve used the word "Lord," she was using the covenant, Savior name of God—Yahweh or Lord—instead of the name of the Creator-God—Elohim.

The next thing we read in Genesis chapter 4 is this: **"Later she gave birth to his brother Abel. Now Abel kept flocks, and Cain worked the soil"** (verse 2). We're not given any information about how many years separated these two sons. The only thing we are told is that Cain grew up to become a farmer and Abel grew up to become a rancher.

"In the course of time Cain brought some of the fruits of the soil as an offering to the Lord. And Abel also brought an offering—fat portions from some of the firstborn of his flock. The Lord looked with favor on Abel and his offering, but on Cain and his offering he did not look with favor. So Cain was very angry, and his face was downcast" (verses 3-5). It's interesting that Cain and Abel gave offerings to the Lord. They obviously learned this from their parents. But how did they learn it? Was it something Adam and Eve decided to do on their own? Possibly. Was it something that the Lord God had told Adam and Eve to do as part of their worship life? That's probably more likely based upon the Lord's future directives to Moses on Mt. Sinai when the Lord God instituted an elaborate system of sacrifices and offerings. But we really don't know for sure.

At any rate, both Cain and Abel made an offering to the Lord. Here again, we see that their offerings were made to the "Lord," the name for God that indicates his free and faithful grace. However, Genesis tells us that the Lord looked with favor on Abel's offering but not Cain's offering. Why was that? The account in Genesis may give us a clue. Did you notice that Cain's offering was described as "some of the fruits of the soil" whereas Abel's offering was described as "fat portions from some of the firstborn of his flock"? The Hebrew word for "fat portions" can mean a particular part of the animal, but it can also mean metaphorically "the very best." So Cain gave just an offering. But Abel gave an offering of the very best that he had.

The New Testament also gives us some clues as to the difference in these two offerings. The writer to the Hebrews, in the "great faith" chapter," tells us: **"By faith Abel brought God a better offering than Cain did. By faith he was commended as righteous, when God spoke well of his offerings. And by faith Abel still speaks, even though he is dead"** (11:4). So here is another potential difference between Cain and

Abel's offerings. The writer to the Hebrews indicates that Abel's offering was made in faith and says nothing about the motivation of Cain's offering.

Also, the New Testament writer Jude describes Cain as an ungodly person in the same breath as Balaam, who wanted to curse Israel, and Korah, who rebelled against the leadership of Moses (see Jude 1:11).

It seems, though, that the apostle John gets to the heart of the difference between Cain and Abel's offerings. He wrote, **"Do not be like Cain, who belonged to the evil one and murdered his brother. And why did he murder him? Because his own actions were evil and his brother's were righteous"** (1 John 3:12).

So the difference was a matter of the heart, of attitude and motive. Abel's offering was given from a heart of faith. Cain's was given from a heart of unbelief. Cain belonged to the evil one (Satan). We have the contrast between believer and unbeliever even though they both outwardly gave an offering to the Lord. With the Lord, what's in the heart is the most important thing. The writer to the Hebrews reminds us that **"without faith it is impossible to please God"** (11:6).

Somehow, and we're not told how, Cain knew that his offering did not please the Lord and was not accepted by the Lord. But instead of looking into the mirror of his own heart, he was filled with resentment and became very angry, burning with anger. Cain's heart progressed from a lack of faith to resentment and from resentment to anger.

If you were the Creator of the universe, the God of heaven and earth, and one of your creatures showed such disrespect and dishonor to you, you might be tempted to send a bolt of lightning from the heavens to take him out. But the Lord didn't do that because he is the God of free and faithful grace.

"Then the Lord said to Cain, 'Why are you angry? Why is your face downcast? If you do what is right, will you not be accepted?'" (Genesis 4:6,7). This is another indication of why the Lord didn't accept Cain's offering—what Cain did wasn't right. The Lord continued: "But if you do not do what is right, sin is crouching at your door; it desires to have you, but you must master it" (verse 7). The Lord gave Cain a choice. Cain could repent of his bad attitude and surrender his anger at God and his brother. He could, in repentance, turn away from the sin crouching at the door of his heart. Or he could let sin get the better of him.

These are powerful and insightful words. The word of the Lord demonstrates the relationship between the attitude of a sinful heart and the potential resulting sinful actions that can come from it. The phrase "crouching at your door" is so descriptive. Think of a Siberian tiger that is crouched down, ready to pounce and kill. That's the picture the Lord painted for Cain. "Your resentment and anger, Cain, is crouching at the door of your heart. It desires to have you, all of you. You can't let that happen. You must master it. You must keep it in check."

In ancient Semitic literature, the verb translated as "lying" or "crouching" was also used to describe demons that the ancients believed guarded entrances or doorways to buildings. The verb suggests that Satan uses the anger of the heart to lead one to take the next step. Sadly, Cain rejected the Lord's warning. The sin that was crouching at the door of his heart sprang into evil action. **"Now Cain said to his brother Abel, 'Let's go out to the field.' While they were in the field, Cain attacked his brother Abel and killed him"** (Genesis 4:8).

I have a couple of questions for you. Do you think I am capable of murder? I am. Do you think you are capable of murder? You are. If we allow sinful attitudes to set up shop in our hearts, we're capable of anything. When we do not master our sinful thoughts, as the Lord God encouraged Cain, Satan will use those thoughts to turn them into sinful actions. The apostle Peter warns us: **"Be alert and of sober mind. Your enemy the devil prowls around like a roaring lion looking for someone to devour. Resist him, standing firm in the faith"** (1 Peter 5:8,9). Resist the devil by resisting the ungodly thoughts of your heart.

Do you recall the time when the religious leaders of Jesus' day criticized his disciples for eating food without first doing the traditional ceremonial washing? The religious leaders accused the disciples of being unclean, of being defiled. Jesus countered the leaders' claims by saying that our uncleanness, what defiles us, isn't what's on the outside. It's what's on the inside. Jesus said: **"What comes out of a person is what defiles them. For it is from within, out of a person's heart, that evil thoughts come—sexual immorality, theft, murder, adultery, greed, malice, deceit, lewdness, envy, slander, arrogance and folly. All these evils come from inside and defile a person"** (Mark 7:20-23). You and I need to take to heart—no pun intended—what's in our hearts. Because what's hidden in our hearts will eventually show up in our lives.

Cain committed the world's first murder. It started with resentment toward the Lord for not accepting his wrongly motivated sacrifice. That resentment spread to his brother Abel, whose sacrifice was accepted by the Lord. The resentment grew into anger. That anger grew into hatred. That hatred turned into murder, the murder of his younger brother Abel.

So what happened next? **"Then the Lord said to Cain, 'Where is your brother Abel?'"** (Genesis 4:9). I've often wondered what the intent of this question from the Lord was. The Bible doesn't tell us, but it seems to me that this was the Lord, the God of grace, trying to reach Cain's heart one more time and lead him to acknowledge that he murdered his brother, to repent of his heinous crime, and to seek the Lord's mercy. But that didn't happen. Cain responded to the Lord in disrespect, with sheer arrogance, and with an outright lie. I don't know how he said it, but it might have been said smugly: **"'I don't know,' he replied. 'Am I my brother's keeper?'"** (verse 9).

The Lord God now declared his judgment upon Cain: **"What have you done? Listen! Your brother's blood cries out to me from the ground"** (verse 10). Cain thought that killing his brother would silence his brother. But no. Abel's blood kept crying out to the Lord from the ground, wanting justice.

And this was the Lord's punishment: **"Now you are under a curse and driven from the ground, which** opened its mouth to receive your brother's blood from your hand. When you work the ground, it will no longer yield its crops for you. You will be a restless wanderer on the earth" (verses 11,12). Even with the Lord pronouncing a curse, this was not eternal condemnation of Cain. Cain could still acknowledge his wrongdoing, repent, and seek forgiveness. The Lord's curse would be a lifelong reminder to Cain of what he did to Abel. Cain would no longer be able to produce a living from being a farmer. He would become a wanderer who would struggle to make a living.

These words apparently got Cain's attention. He responded by saying: **"My punishment is more than I can bear. Today you are driving me from the land, and I will be hidden from your presence; I will be a restless wanderer on the earth, and whoever finds me will kill me"** (verses 13,14). Cain's response tells us that there still was no regret or remorse, no acknowledgement of his wrongdoing, no repentance. His biggest fear was that someone from among his own relatives would come and take revenge upon him, blood revenge, a life for a life.

Even though Cain didn't deserve the Lord's kindness and grace, the Lord offered it with a promise: **"'Not so; anyone who kills Cain will suffer vengeance seven times over.' Then the LORD put a mark on Cain so that no one who found him would kill him. So Cain went out from the LORD's presence and lived in the land of Nod, east of Eden"** (verses 15,16).

What was this mark that the Lord placed on Cain? The Hebrew word can mean "a sign, a token, a pledge, or a symbol." Some Bible scholars think it was a visible mark on his body, like a tattoo. Other scholars think it was a visible miracle like God gave to Moses. One of the signs that Moses was to become the leader of the people of Israel was that he could throw his staff on the ground and it would become a snake.

Or think about Hezekiah's sign that he would recover from his illness and live 15 additional years. The Lord said, **"I will make the shadow cast by the sun go back the ten steps it has gone down on the stairway of Ahaz"** (Isaiah 38:8). That sign required God to reverse the rotation of the earth. The sign that the Lord gave to Cain could have been a miraculous sign, but we just don't know for sure. We do know it represented the Lord's promise that Cain would not be murdered like he murdered his brother Abel.

Cain left the presence of the Lord and went to live as a nomad in the land of Nod, east of the Garden of Eden. He suffered the consequences of not acknowledging or repenting of his sin of murder. The Bible tells us very little about Cain. We know he took a wife and had a son and descendants.

Cain is one example of true crime in the Bible. He was the first murderer. We've seen how the Lord responded to Cain who demonstrated his unbelief. For you and me, the big takeaway is the nature of sin that may be crouching at the door of our hearts. If we want to learn from Cain, we need to take sin seriously. We need to resist it, repent of it, and ask for God's strength to deal with it, no matter what it is.

If we don't, we risk having what's hidden in our hearts showing up in our lives.

MOSES

As we continue with these ten crimes, recall that we're exploring them from three different perspectives. First, we want to look at who did it and why; second, how God responded to the person who committed the crime; and third, what we can learn from it. We're going to discover two different threads among these criminals in the Bible. One thread includes those who were believers in the true God, Yahweh. The other thread includes those who weren't.

In this chapter, we will investigate another murder, a murder committed by Moses. I should also point out that a case can be made for saying that Moses didn't commit murder, even though he willfully ended the life of an Egyptian slave master. We'll unpack both perspectives as we look at this event in Moses' life.

Let's start with the details of this event recorded in Exodus chapter 2:

One day, after Moses had grown up, he went out to where his own people were and watched them at their hard labor. He saw an Egyptian

beating a Hebrew, one of his own people. Looking this way and that and seeing no one, he killed the Egyptian and hid him in the sand. The next day he went out and saw two Hebrews fighting. He asked the one in the wrong, "Why are you hitting your fellow Hebrew?"

The man said, "Who made you ruler and judge over us? Are you thinking of killing me as you killed the Egyptian?" Then Moses was afraid and thought, "What I did must have become known."

When Pharaoh heard of this, he tried to kill Moses, but Moses fled from Pharaoh and went to live in Midian. (verses 11-15)

There are two Hebrew words we want to take a closer look at in these verses. One word is translated as "beating" and the other as "killing" or "killed." The challenge for us is that Hebrew words often have a wide range of meanings. For example, the Hebrew word translated as "beating" is pronounced *naw-caw*. It can mean "to strike a person with a fist or with a weapon or tool in one's hand." But *naw-caw* can also mean "to kill." So when Moses saw an Egyptian slave master beating a Hebrew slave, did Moses witness the Hebrew being beaten or being killed? The Hebrew word would allow for either. More on this in a bit.

This same word, *naw-caw*, is also used when we are

told that Moses "killed" the Egyptian and hid him in the sand. The fact that Moses hid the Egyptian in the sand definitely warrants, in this particular verse, to translate *naw-caw* as "killed."

Now *naw-caw* occurs one more time in these verses. The next day Moses went out among the Hebrew people and saw two men fighting. We're told that Moses asked the man who started the fight, **"Why are you hitting [or beating] your fellow Hebrew?"** (Exodus 2:13). Was this man beating his fellow Hebrew with his fist or with a tool in his hand? Or was he in the process of beating him to death? The Hebrew word allows for either.

The man whom Moses confronted with his question responded back, **"Who made you ruler and judge over us? Are you thinking of killing me as you killed the Egyptian?"** (Exodus 2:14). The Hebrew man did not use the word *naw-caw*. He used a different Hebrew word pronounced *haw-rag*. This word means "to kill or slay," but it has a specific shade of meaning. It means "to kill with ruthless violence," especially violence done privately. So the Hebrew man asked Moses, "Are you thinking of killing me as you privately and ruthlessly killed the Egyptian?"

The word *kill* occurs one more time in this section: **"When Pharaoh heard of this, he tried to kill Moses, but Moses fled from Pharaoh and went to live in Midian"** (verse 15). The word for "kill" that Pharaoh used was the same word the Hebrew man used—*haw-rag*—"to kill ruthlessly, with vengeance." So in this section, we have an Egyptian either beating or killing a Hebrew slave, Moses killing the Egyptian, a Hebrew man wondering if Moses was going to kill him like he killed the Egyptian, and Pharaoh seeking to have Moses killed because he killed an Egyptian. There's a whole lot of killing going on here!

This story about Moses got me thinking about another story in Moses' life: when Moses went up Mt. Sinai to receive the Ten Commandments. One of God's commandments forbids murder. So what word did the Lord use in his commandment: *You shall not murder*? Was it *naw-caw*, the word translated as "beating" but can also mean "to end the life of someone"; or was it *haw-rag*, the word meaning "to kill someone ruthlessly or with personal vengeance"? Guess what? Neither. The Lord God used a different Hebrew word in the commandment: *ra-tsach*. I mentioned earlier that some Hebrew words have a range of meanings. That's also true of *ra-tsach*.

Its basic meaning is "to murder, slay, or kill." But on the one end of the word-meaning spectrum, *ra-tsach* is used to describe an accidental killing, like if one of your bulls got out of its pen and gored another man to death. That would be an accidental killing. However, on the other end of the word-meaning spectrum, *ra-tsach* can refer to premeditated, first-degree murder. It can also refer to the act of avenging the death of another person. It can also mean to assassinate someone. So does the word *ra-tsach* in the murder commandment refer to unintentional killing or murder or both?

I believe there's an answer. In the New Testament, the commandment forbidding murder shows up six times: twice in Matthew's gospel, once each in Mark's and Luke's gospel accounts, once in Romans, and once in James. In all six places, the Greek word *phoneuo* is used. The definition for *phoneuo* is "to deprive a person of life by illegal, intentional killing"—"to murder, to commit murder." All told, the word *phoneuo* occurs 12 times in the New Testament, with all 12 occurrences referring to murder. The authors of the New Testament saw the commandment forbidding murder to be just that—the illegal, intentional killing of another human being.

It's also worth mentioning that in the Lord's Old Testament laws there were different punishments for whether ending a human life was unintentional or accidental or whether it was premeditated. When it came to premeditated murder, the Lord required the guilty party to be put to death. Today, we would call it capital punishment. In the case of unintentional or accidental death, the punishment was less than a life for a life. One final point, the word *ra-tsach* is never used in the Bible to describe the killing that occurs in war.

With that background on word meanings, let's get back to what Moses did. Was Moses' killing of the Egyptian intentional? It certainly wasn't accidental, so yes, it was intentional. Was it illegal? Based upon Pharaoh's response to hearing about this dead Egyptian, Pharaoh considered it illegal and worthy of capital punishment. After all, Pharaoh made the rules in Egypt. So from Pharaoh's perspective, this was murder.

Moses' actions confirmed that he knew it was wrong

to take the life of this Egyptian. Before he actually killed the Egyptian, he checked out his surroundings to make sure no one would see him do it. **"Looking this way and that and seeing no one, he killed the Egyptian"** (Exodus 2:12). And then Moses sought to cover up the Egyptian's death by hiding him in the sand. So it seems we have a murder and a cover-up. Then, to escape Pharaoh's threat to his own life, Moses fled Egypt and went to live in Midian.

Where then does this idea come from that Moses' killing of this Egyptian wasn't necessarily a murder? I think it's an interesting question. There are two places in the Bible, both in the New Testament, that give us some additional insight into Moses' killing of the Egyptian. One is in Acts chapter 7, and the other is in Hebrews chapter 11.

Acts chapter 6 introduces us to Stephen, who is described as **"a man full of God's grace and power,"** who **"performed great wonders and signs among the people"** (verse 8). Opposition to Stephen arose from a group of religious leaders known as the Synagogue of the Freedmen. These leaders secretly persuaded others to accuse Stephen of blasphemy against Moses and against God. Acts chapter 7 then records Stephen's defense before the Sanhedrin of this charge of blasphemy. In Stephen's defense address, he recounted Old Testament events beginning with Abraham, Isaac, and Jacob, then continued with Moses and Aaron, and concluded with David and Solomon.

Here is what Stephen said about Moses and his killing of the Egyptian. As you read these words of Stephen, look for new information that you didn't learn from the Exodus account of this event:

At that time Moses was born, and he was no ordinary child. For three months he was cared for by his family. When he was placed outside, Pharaoh's daughter took him and brought him up as her own son. Moses was educated in all the wisdom of the Egyptians and was powerful in speech and action. When Moses was forty years old, he decided to visit his own people, the Israelites. He saw one of them being mistreated by an Egyptian, so he went to his defense and avenged him by killing the Egyptian. Moses thought that his own people would realize that God was using him to rescue them, but they did not. (Acts 7:20-25)

Some of what Stephen said we know from Exodus chapter 2. Pharaoh had ordered that all boys born to Hebrew women were to be killed. Let's just pause right there. Tucked away in the story of Moses' birth is one of the most heinous types of crimes in history, genocide. Pharaoh had ordered the death of all Hebrew boys. Why? Pharaoh lived with the fear that the Hebrews were getting too numerous and too powerful. They were becoming a threat to the nation of Egypt.

Moses was born, and his mother hid him for three months. When she and her husband couldn't hide him any longer, she put the little one in a tar-pitched basket and put the basket among the reeds of the Nile at a location where Pharaoh's daughter came to bathe. It was actually Pharaoh's daughter who named this baby boy Moses. His name means "I drew him out of water."

Now Stephen also gives us some new information. He said that Moses was educated in the wisdom of the Egyptians and was powerful in speech and action. We also learn that the Exodus chapter 2 event happened when Moses was 40 years old. Here's another insight: Moses saw that his fellow Hebrew was being *mistreated* by an Egyptian, as Stephen described it. Remember when I mentioned that the Hebrew word translated as "beating" could either be "beating" or "killing"? Stephen clarified this for us. The Hebrew slave was being mistreated by his Egyptian slave master, not killed. "**[Moses] went to [the man's] defense and avenged him by killing the Egyptian**" (Acts 7:24).

We also learn from Stephen about Moses' thought process for killing the Egyptian. Did you catch it? "**Moses thought that his own people would realize that God was using him to rescue them, but they did not**" (Acts 7:25). Stephen didn't tell us how Moses came to understand that God was going to use him to rescue God's chosen people, just that he knew it. But Moses' timetable for rescuing God's people and the Lord God's timetable were 40 years apart. Moses wouldn't return from Midian to be Israel's rescuer until he was 80 years old.

Moses had made his own assumptions about his role as rescuer. As a result, he took matters into his own hands and killed the Egyptian. The Lord God did not tell Moses to do it. Moses acted on his own, and as a result, he had to flee from Egypt until the Lord was ready for him to lead.

Here's one of the big takeaways for us from what Moses did. We need to remember that the Lord has his own timetable and plans. Like Moses, we can find ourselves in a difficult position if we try to impose our own timetables and plans instead of waiting for the Lord to reveal his plans and his timetable. For us, that is often very hard to do.

There are some additional insights we learn from what the writer to the Hebrews says about these events in Moses' life. Again, note the new insights learned here:

> **By faith Moses' parents hid him for three months after he was born, because they saw he was no ordinary child, and they were not afraid of the king's edict. By faith Moses, when he had grown up, refused to be known as the son of Pharaoh's daughter. He chose to be mistreated along with the people of God rather than to enjoy the fleeting pleasures of sin. He regarded disgrace for the sake of Christ as of greater value than the treasures of Egypt, because he was looking ahead to his reward. (11:23-26)**

Did you catch the new insights? Moses' parents had great faith. They did not fear Pharaoh's edict to kill all the male babies. Here's another one: when Moses had grown up, he refused to be known as the son of Pharaoh's daughter. He sided with his own people, those who were slaves of Pharaoh and being mistreated. Moses gave up the riches and the pleasures that could be had living in Pharaoh's palace and a member of his family. Moses considered the promises of God's reward to be worth so much more. This is a second takeaway for us. The wealth, privilege, honor, and power that our culture and world offer can't compare with the eternal glory, honor, and riches that are ours because of Jesus.

Forty years after Moses fled Egypt to Midian, the Lord God showed up one day in a burning bush that didn't burn up. The Lord called Moses to return to Egypt to lead his people out of Egypt. Moses was quite reluctant to go but eventually did. It was now the Lord's timetable and plan to have Moses rescue God's people from the land of Egypt and the oppression of Pharaoh. Now Moses got on board with God's plan.

What's the difference between Moses killing the Egyptian and Cain killing his brother Abel? One word—*faith*. Moses acted by faith. Although it was not in alignment with the Lord's plan, he did act in faith. Cain lacked faith in the Lord. And because of faith or lack thereof, the end results for Cain and Moses were incredibly different.

Cain was cursed. Moses was blessed.

KING DAVID

In this chapter, we're going to look at another murder, a murder committed by King David. This crime was much more involved than just the ending of another man's life. That's because another crime preceded the crime of murder. In this story, there's a wealth of dialogue between various characters. This story of King David, found in 2 Samuel chapters 11 and 12, is one of the most detailed accounts of any crime recorded in the Bible. There's lots to unpack, so let's get started.

Second Samuel chapter 11 begins: **"In the spring, at the time when kings go off to war, David sent Joab out with the king's men and the whole Israelite army. They destroyed the Ammonites and besieged Rabbah. But David remained in Jerusalem"** (verse 1).

In the ancient Middle Eastern world, kings would wait until spring to wage war. There were two main reasons. From about October to March, it was much colder, and it was also the rainy season. Rain made travel for an army much more difficult.

We read that David sent Joab and his army to fight against the Ammonites. So first of all, who's Joab? Joab was the commander of David's army. Today, he would have the rank of army general. Joab was also David's nephew, the son of David's sister Zeruiah. Joab was an interesting military man. He was both loyal and disloyal to King David during his tenure as the general of David's army. More on Joab in a bit.

Who were the Ammonites and why was King David going to war against them? There's an interesting backstory I'd like to share with you. First, the Ammonites were descendants of Lot, Abraham's nephew. They lived east of the Jordan River, about one hundred miles northeast of Jerusalem.

Saul (the very first king of Israel and the king before David) encountered the Ammonites at a border town by the name of Jabesh-Gilead. The Ammonites, under the leadership of Nahash, had laid siege to the city. The leaders of the city asked for a treaty with the Ammonites to avoid Nahash destroying the town and killing all the people. The townsfolk would agree to be Nahash's subjects. Nahash's response to this request was a bit bizarre. Nahash said he would be happy to make a treaty with the people with the condition that he could gouge out the right eye of every person living in Jabesh-Gilead. When King Saul heard about the siege and Nahash's treaty terms, he gathered his army and headed to the besieged city. In a brilliant military move, King Saul defeated the Ammonites and rescued the city of Jabesh-Gilead.

Now fast-forward to King David's reign. In the

course of time, the king of the Ammonites died and his son Hanun succeeded him as king. David thought, **"I will show kindness to Hanun son of Nahash, just as his father showed kindness to me"** (2 Samuel 10:2).

We don't know for sure what the kindness was that Nahash had shown to David. Perhaps it was protection from their shared enemy, King Saul? We really don't know. David sent a delegation to Hanun to express his sympathy to Hanun at the death of his father. This was a customary practice in ancient times. But upon their arrival, the Ammonite nobles convinced their new king, Hanun, that the men in this delegation from David were actually spies. Hanun bought into this spy theory. Then he did something bizarre. Hanun humiliated the men of the delegation. I'm not going to describe the graphic details here. You can read them for yourself in 2 Samuel chapter 10. But make no mistake, the men of the delegation were humiliated.

The Ammonites soon learned that because they had humiliated David's delegation, they had become a rancid stench in David's nostrils. That's an interesting analogy, don't you think? They figured that David might show up on their doorstep with his army. So they went out and hired 33,000 mercenary soldiers, the majority of them being Arameans (also known as Syrians). David didn't show up with his army; he instead sent Joab to lead the Israelite army.

The Ammonite army came out of their fortified city, and the mercenary soldier army came at the Israelite army from the open country, sandwiching Joab and his troops. So Joab split the army in half, one half to fight the Ammonites and other half to fight the mercenary army. As the battle raged, the mercenary army saw that they were losing, so they turned tail and ran. When the Ammonites saw that the mercenaries were fleeing, they retreated back behind the fortified walls of their city. The Israelite army survived, but they weren't victorious. They wouldn't be victorious until David came and led his army against the mercenary army, the Arameans. Yet they still had the Ammonites to deal with.

My reason for sharing this backstory is to illustrate that when David led his army, they were victorious. That's what kings were supposed to do. That's what the Lord wanted David to be doing.

But as we read at the beginning of this chapter, **"David sent Joab out with the king's men and the whole Israelite army. They destroyed the Ammonites and besieged Rabbah. But David remained in Jerusalem"** (2 Samuel 11:1). For this military campaign, David again didn't lead his army. Joab was successful in defeating some of the Ammonites, but they had not captured the fortified city of Rabbah, known today as Amman, Jordan. Think of that. David sent Joab to lead the fight while he remained back at the palace enjoying the comforts of home. It was an unwise decision with lifelong, tragic consequences.

One evening David got up from his bed and

walked around the roof of the palace. From the roof he saw a woman bathing. The woman was very beautiful, and David sent someone to find out about her. The man said, "She is Bathsheba, the daughter of Eliam and the wife of Uriah the Hittite." Then David sent messengers to get her. She came to him, and he slept with her. . . . Then she went back home. The woman conceived and sent word to David, saying, "I am pregnant." (2 Samuel 11:2-5)

Not only was Bathsheba married; she was married to Uriah, one of David's most trusted soldiers, one of his "mighty men." And Eliam, Bathsheba's father, was also one of David's mighty men. David's mighty men were a group of 30 elite warriors. David knew both of them well. And in addition, Bathsheba's grandfather, whose name was Ahithophel, was one of David's chief counselors in his inner circle.

We shouldn't forget to mention that King David was also married. In fact, he had taken multiple wives. What David and Bathsheba did was not a consensual affair. It was adultery. And according to God's Old Testament law, the punishment for adultery was death. For years, David had not honored God's plan for marriage of one man, one woman. David's actions on this day did not honor his Lord either.

I'm reminded of the words of the apostle Paul in his letter to the churches in Galatia. He said, **"So I say, live** by the Spirit, and you will not gratify the desires of the sinful flesh. For the flesh desires what is contrary to the Spirit, and the Spirit what is contrary to the flesh. They are in conflict with each other"** (Galatians 5:16,17). David had surrendered himself to his own sinful desires.

When word came to David that Bathsheba was pregnant, he hatched a cover-up:

> **David sent word to Joab: "Send me Uriah the Hittite." And Joab sent him to David. When Uriah came to him, David asked him how Joab was, how the soldiers were and how the war was going. Then David said to Uriah, "Go down to your house and wash your feet." So Uriah left the palace, and a gift from the king was sent after him. But Uriah slept at the entrance to the palace with all his master's servants and did not go down to his house."** (2 Samuel 11:6-9)

The next morning, David asked Uriah why he didn't go home. Uriah's response showed his own personal integrity and respect for his fellow soldiers. Uriah said to David, **"The ark and Israel and Judah are staying in tents, and my commander Joab and my lord's men are camped in the open country. How could I go to my house to eat and drink and make love to my wife? As surely as you live, I will not do such a thing!"** (2 Samuel 11:11).

The contrast in honor and duty and integrity

between Uriah and David could not have been greater. David's cover-up hit a snag. So David told Uriah to stay one more day. That evening, David invited Uriah to dinner and drinks. In fact, David got Uriah drunk in the hopes his honorable heart would be softened and he would go home to his wife, but he didn't. David's cover-up hit another snag.

The next morning David wrote a letter to Joab. It was a letter sealing Uriah's fate. It was a letter that Uriah would personally carry back to his commander. The letter said, **"Put Uriah out in front where the fighting is fiercest. Then withdraw from him so he will be struck down and die"** (2 Samuel 11:15). And Joab did. Uriah died in battle along with some other soldiers. David's cover-up cost the lives of his own soldiers. Adultery, lies, cover-up, and murder.

"When Uriah's wife heard that her husband was dead, she mourned for him. After the time of mourning was over, David had her brought to his house, and she became his wife and bore him a son. But the thing David had done displeased the Lord" (2 Samuel 11:26,27).

David kept the cover-up going for a year or so. He never confessed the crimes he had committed. Nothing is mentioned in 2 Samuel about David's heart and soul at this time, but we do get some insight from a psalm that David wrote later. In Psalm 32, David wrote:

Blessed is the one whose transgressions are forgiven, whose sins are covered. Blessed is the

one whose sin the Lord does not count against them and in whose spirit is no deceit. When I kept silent, my bones wasted away through my groaning all day long. For day and night your hand was heavy on me; my strength was sapped as in the heat of summer. (Psalm 32:1-4)

When David failed to confess his crime and his sin against God, his life became miserable. But he didn't listen to his conscience nor act upon it. There was stress, agony, and a lack of joy in his life. According to what David wrote in Psalm 32, his heart and soul were spiraling downward out of control. The Lord, who is so gracious and compassionate, was not going to let his chosen servant David go down this path any longer.

So the Lord sent the prophet Nathan to David. David knew Nathan well. Earlier, Nathan had delivered a wonderful message of blessing about David and his descendants. David was told that the Savior of the world would come from his descendants. On this particular day, Nathan didn't bring a message of blessing; rather, he brought one of rebuke.

Nathan told David:

"There were two men in a certain town, one rich and the other poor. The rich man had a very large number of sheep and cattle, but the poor man had nothing except one little ewe lamb he had bought. He raised it, and it grew up with him and his children. It shared his food, drank from his cup and even slept in his arms. It was like a daughter to him.

"Now a traveler came to the rich man, but the rich man refrained from taking one of his own sheep or cattle to prepare a meal for the traveler who had come to him. Instead, he took the ewe lamb that belonged to the poor man and prepared it for the one who had come to him."

David burned with anger against the man and said to Nathan, "As surely as the Lord lives, the man who did this must die! He must pay for that lamb four times over, because he did such a thing and had no pity."

Then Nathan said to David, "You are the man!"
(2 Samuel 12:1-7)

Nathan then went on to remind David that the Lord God of Israel had anointed him king and protected him from King Saul who had tried to kill him. The Lord had given the throne to David over all Israel and Judah. If that were not enough, the Lord would have given him more. **"Why did you despise the word of the Lord by doing what is evil in his eyes?"** (2 Samuel 12:9).

Then Nathan shared the consequences that would come to David and his family. The sword would never depart from David's life; family would murder family. Also, some of David's wives would be taken by other family members, just to spite David and to satisfy their own sexual desires.

David was convicted of his crimes of adultery and murder.

> Then David said to Nathan, "I have sinned against the Lord."
>
> Nathan replied, "The Lord has taken away your sin. You are not going to die. But because by doing this you have shown utter contempt for the Lord, the son born to you will die."
> (2 Samuel 12:13,14)

David wrote another psalm that reflected on this "come to Jesus" meeting with Nathan. It's Psalm 51, which is a psalm of repentance, forgiveness, and restoration. It's worth reading these words of David because they're a window into his heart and soul.

> Have mercy on me, O God, according to your unfailing love; according to your great compassion blot out my transgressions. Wash away all my iniquity and cleanse me from my sin.
>
> For I know my transgressions, and my sin is always before me. Against you, you only, have

I sinned and done what is evil in your sight; so you are right in your verdict and justified when you judge. Surely I was sinful at birth, sinful from the time my mother conceived me. Yet you desired faithfulness even in the womb; you taught me wisdom in that secret place.

Cleanse me with hyssop, and I will be clean; wash me, and I will be whiter than snow. Let me hear joy and gladness; let the bones you have crushed rejoice. Hide your face from my sins and blot out all my iniquity.

Create in me a pure heart, O God, and renew a steadfast spirit within me. Do not cast me from your presence or take your Holy Spirit from me. Restore to me the joy of your salvation and grant me a willing spirit, to sustain me. (verses 1-12)

After David's day of repentance, forgiveness, and restoration, he went out to lead his army to capture the city of Rabbah. The Lord blessed him with victory.

So here's a question for you. Have you ever heard David described as "a man after God's own heart"? It seems like a contradiction after hearing about David's crimes of adultery and murder.

This phrase originated with the prophet Samuel. We need to back up to when Saul was king. King Saul had usurped the role of the priest by offering a burnt sacrifice. According to God's Old Testament law, kings were not permitted to serve in the role as priest.

So Samuel said to Saul: **"You have done a foolish thing. . . . You have not kept the command the L**ORD **your God gave you; if you had, he would have established your kingdom over Israel for all time. But now your kingdom will not endure; the L**ORD **has sought out a man after his own heart and appointed him ruler of his people, because you have not kept the L**ORD**'s command"** (1 Samuel 13:13,14).

The apostle Paul in the New Testament also described David this way in the book of Acts. Paul had delivered a message to the people living in the city in Antioch, a town that was located in what is present-day Turkey. Paul recalled some Old Testament history: **"After removing Saul, he made David their king. God testified concerning him, 'I have found David son of Jesse, a man after my own heart; he will do everything I want him to do.' From this man's descendants God has brought to Israel the Savior Jesus, as he promised"** (Acts 13:22,23).

So what made David a man after God's own heart despite his crimes? First of all, David had absolute faith and trust in God. Think of David fearlessly killing the Philistine giant, Goliath. At that time, David said, **"The L**ORD **who rescued me from the paw of the lion and the paw of the bear will rescue me from the hand of this Philistine"** (1 Samuel 17:37).

Or think of David and the many psalms he wrote. In the psalms, David repeatedly speaks of loving the law of God. He wrote, **"For I delight in your commands because I love them. I reach out for your commands, which I love, that I may meditate on your decrees"** (Psalm 119:47,48).

Or think of the thankfulness that David expressed. In Psalm 100, David wrote:

Shout for joy to the Lord, all the earth. Worship the Lord with gladness; come before him with joyful songs. Know that the Lord is God. It is he who made us, and we are his; we are his people, the sheep of his pasture.

Enter his gates with thanksgiving and his courts with praise; give thanks to him and praise his name. For the Lord is good and his love endures forever; his faithfulness continues through all generations. (verses 1-5)

That's a man—criminal though he was—after God's own heart.

There are a couple of big takeaways for us from this story of David. First, we need to be self-aware that we are all capable of committing the same crimes of adultery and murder as David did. We never want to think that we are so strong in our faith that we would never fall as David fell. Remember, **"if you think you are standing firm, be**

careful that you don't fall!" (1 Corinthians 10:12).

Second, when we fail to confess the wrongs we have done, it will affect our hearts, souls, and minds. Unconfessed sin weighs heavily on the human soul and negatively affects our relationship with our Savior.

Third, there is no sin, no mistake, no treachery, no crime that is too great for the Lord God to forgive. Jesus died on a cross to take away all sin, and the key word is *all*.

And finally, we ought to pursue being a man or woman after God's own heart—trusting God, studying his Word, and being thankful for his blessings.

KING DAVID'S FAMILY

In the previous chapter, we learned how the prophet Nathan confronted King David with his crimes of adultery and murder. Nathan also prophesied to David about other consequences that would come to him and his family because of his disobedience: **"This is what the Lord says: 'Out of your own household I am going to bring calamity on you. Before your very eyes I will take your wives and give them to one who is close to you, and he will sleep with your wives in broad daylight. You did it in secret, but I will do this thing in broad daylight before all Israel'"** (2 Samuel 12:11,12).

In this chapter, we begin to see those consequences play out as we examine the crimes committed by members of David's family. Let's start with Joab, the general of David's army. Recall that Joab was family. He was King David's nephew.

Joab appeared on the scene when David became the ruler of Judah. David became Judah's king after the death of King Saul and three of his sons: Jonathan, Abinadab, and Malki-Shua. The northern region of Israel did not accept David as king. Instead, they anointed one of Saul's remaining sons, Ish-Bosheth, to be king in the north. Ish-Bosheth was 40 years old when he became king.

In 2 Samuel chapter 2, we read about a battle at Gibeon, a town located about one hundred miles northwest of Jerusalem. In this battle, David's men were victorious over Ish-Bosheth's army led by Abner, who had long been King Saul's general. Also at this battle were Joab and his two brothers, Abishai and Asahel. Near the end of the battle, as Abner's soldiers were retreating, Asahel pursued General Abner. Abner called out to Asahel, **"Stop chasing me! Why should I strike you down? How could I look your brother Joab in the face?"** (2 Samuel 2:22). But Asahel did not stop his pursuit of Abner. Reluctantly, Abner turned to confront Asahel and killed him by thrusting the butt of his spear into Asahel's stomach. Now Joab would never forget who it was that killed his brother. From that day forward, Joab looked for an opportunity to avenge Asahel's death.

The conflict between the house of Saul and the house of David lasted a long time, more than seven years. As time went on, David grew stronger and stronger, and the house of Saul grew weaker and weaker. Then something happened that caused General Abner to switch his allegiance from King Ish-Bosheth to King David.

One day Ish-Bosheth accused Abner of sleeping with one of King Saul's concubines. A concubine was a woman in a polygamous royal marriage who had less status than one of the king's actual wives. A second-class wife, you might say. It was a false accusation, and because of it, Abner swore an oath to transfer the house of Saul in the north to the house of David in the south so that David would be king over all Israel and Judah. Abner then headed south to meet with King David in Hebron to offer his allegiance. David accepted the offer, and Abner returned to the north to rally the army and the people to accept David as their king.

Just as Abner left Hebron, Joab returned to Hebron from plundering a town. When Joab learned that Abner had come to Hebron and that David had accepted Abner's offer and sent him away in peace, Joab was angry. Joab accused Abner of being deceptive and trying to find out what King David's plans were.

Then without David's knowledge, Joab sent messengers after Abner and his men and told them to return to Hebron. Abner returned to Hebron. When he arrived, Joab took him aside into an inner chamber, as though he wanted to talk to Abner privately. But Joab didn't want to talk. Instead, he fatally stabbed Abner in the gut. In 2 Samuel chapter 3, we read the summary of this day: **"Joab and his brother Abishai murdered Abner because he had killed their brother Asahel in the battle at Gibeon"** (verse 30). Joab had gotten his revenge.

And David mourned the death of Abner.

The next time we hear about Joab was what we learned about in the previous chapter—David's crimes of adultery with Bathsheba and the murder of Uriah the Hittite. As we discovered, Joab carried out the details of Uriah's death and was complicit in it.

Before we continue with the story of David's nephew Joab, let's uncover the crimes involving three of David's children—Amnon, Tamar, and Absalom. Absalom and Tamar were brother and sister. Amnon was a half brother because, although he was David's son, he was the son of a different mother. Amnon was in love with his half sister Tamar, who was described as being very beautiful. Amnon tried and tried to win the heart of Tamar but was unsuccessful. He became frustrated, so much so that a friend of his noticed how despondent he was. This friend was Jonadab, another of King David's nephews, making him a cousin to Amnon.

Jonadab convinced his cousin to share what was bothering him. When Jonadab heard Amnon's story, he suggested a shrewd but dishonest plan: **"Go to bed and pretend to be ill. . . . When your father comes to see you, say to him, 'I would like my sister Tamar to come and give me something to eat. Let her prepare the food in my sight so I may watch her and then eat it from her hand'"** (2 Samuel 13:5). Long story short, the plan unfolded as Jonadab had devised it. When Tamar brought the food into Amnon's bedroom, he grabbed her. When Tamar resisted, Amnon raped her.

Amnon's pursuit of Tamar's love now turned into sheer hatred for her. He hated her more than he had loved her, so we are told. Amnon told her to get out. In fact, he had her thrown out. Tamar left and went to her brother Absalom. Tamar ended up living in Absalom's home as a desolate and disgraced woman. Absalom didn't say anything to Amnon about his crime. He didn't confront him, at least not for the next two years.

Two years later, when Absalom's sheepshearers were shearing sheep near Jerusalem, Absalom invited his father and all his brothers to come there. King David declined but gave Absalom his blessing. Absalom specifically requested that Amnon come, which David questioned. In the end, all of David's sons went to visit their brother Absalom. At this sheepshearing party, Absalom instructed his men to wait until Amnon had plenty to drink and was in high spirits and then to kill him, which they did. Absalom murdered his brother Amnon because Amnon had raped his sister Tamar. It was a crime two years in the making.

When Amnon was dead, all the other sons of David got on their mules and headed back to Jerusalem. People tend not to stick around crime scenes. While they were on their way home, a messenger brought a report to David that Absalom had murdered *all* the king's sons. Before he was totally overwhelmed with grief, however, Jonadab, Amnon's cousin, reported to his Uncle David what actually happened. Only Amnon was murdered.

And David mourned the death of Amnon.

After Absalom had murdered Amnon, he fled to Geshur, a region in Israel on the east side of the Jordan River. The people who lived there were known as the Geshurites, a group of Canaanite people who were allowed to remain after Joshua divided the land into the 12 tribes. Today this region is known as the Golan Heights. Absalom likely fled to Geshur because it was the hometown of his mother, Maakah. Maakah was the daughter of the Geshurite king whom David had taken to be one of his wives. We learn from 2 Samuel chapter 13 that Absalom stayed in Geshur for three years.

King David mourned for his son Amnon for a time, but he eventually got to the point where he longed to see his wayward but favorite son, Absalom, once again. Joab was well aware that David wanted to see his favorite son, so he devised a ruse with a woman from Tekoa to get King David to pardon Absalom and allow him to return to Jerusalem. David saw through the ruse and instinctively knew that Joab was behind it. Even so, David instructed Joab to bring Absalom back to Jerusalem, which he did immediately. However, it would be another two years before David and Absalom were reunited and reconciled.

As time went on, Absalom developed a real thirst for power, influence, and popularity. He acquired for himself a chariot with horses and paraded around town with 50 men who accompanied him. He'd also get up early and stand by the road leading into the city. If people had an issue they wanted a king's official to resolve, Absalom would tell them there wasn't anyone to hear their concerns. He followed that up with a claim that things would be different if he were a judge in Israel. Absalom began to undermine his father's authority and began to win the hearts of the people of Israel by pretending he cared for them. Absalom reminds me of a power-hungry, shrewd politician, which I guess he was.

Absalom conspired against his father, built up an army, and instituted a propaganda campaign to win the hearts of people, so much so that people throughout Israel declared Absalom to be king in Hebron, a city just 20 miles south of Jerusalem. When word came to King David that the hearts of the men of Israel were with Absalom, David and those loyal to him fled the city of Jerusalem. As David fled the city, he experienced a low point in his life. He was cursed by a member of Saul's clan named Shimei who also pelted David with rocks and dirt. King David was on the run.

There are two men I should also mention, men who deserted David to serve Absalom. One was Ahithophel, whom we met in the previous chapter. Ahithophel was David's chief advisor, and recall he was the grandfather of Bathsheba. The Bible doesn't tell us his motives for abandoning the king, but it seems reasonable that he harbored anger and resentment because of what David did to his granddaughter and to her husband, Uriah.

The other man whom I want to mention was a personal friend of David's, a man by the name of Hushai. When Absalom asked Hushai why he had abandoned his friend David, Hushai revealed that just as he had served David, so now he wanted to serve the son. **"Then Hushai the Arkite, David's confidant, went to Absalom and said to him, 'Long live the king! Long live the king!'"** (2 Samuel 16:16). Hushai seems to have been looking out for himself and his future political career.

We do get a bit of a window into Ahithophel's heart when Absalom asked him to give him his best advice. Ahithophel said, **"'Sleep with your father's concubines whom he left to take care of the palace. Then all Israel will hear that you made yourself obnoxious to your father, and the hands of everyone with you will be resolute.' So they pitched a tent for Absalom on the roof, and he slept with his father's concubines in the sight of all Israel"** (2 Samuel 16:21,22).

Do you recall that the prophet Nathan specifically said this would happen? And there's a tinge of irony, don't you think, that Absalom committed these acts of sexual revenge on the very same rooftop that David had first observed Bathsheba bathing?

Absalom also asked Ahithophel for a battle strategy against David and his men. Ahithophel suggested an immediate strike against David—kill him and spare the lives of all who were with him. Seemed like a good plan. But then Absalom asked for a battle strategy from Hushai. Hushai advised taking some time to recruit more soldiers from all over Israel and then going after David.

What happened next is a window into Hushai's heart. In the event that Absalom would go with Ahithophel's advice to hit David hard and hit him that very day, Hushai sent two priests to find David and warn him to cross over the Jordan River immediately. David and his men crossed the Jordan and headed to a place called Mahanaim near the Jabbock River.

What Hushai did in sending the two priests to find David revealed that he was still loyal to David and was acting as a friend and as a double agent. God used Hushai to frustrate the advice of Ahithophel. **"When Ahithophel saw that his advice had not been followed, he saddled his donkey and set out for his house in his hometown. He put his house in order and then hanged himself"** (2 Samuel 17:23). Add suicide to the growing list of tragic events.

Absalom and his men had pursued David across the Jordan River and camped in Gilead, not too far from David and his men. David prepared his army to attack Absalom. He divided his army into three battalions with Joab leading one battalion; Abishai, Joab's brother, leading the second battalion; and Ittai the Gittite, the third battalion.

David's plan was to march out with his generals, but they advised him not to. The risk was too great that he would be captured and killed. Because the only thing Absalom really wanted was to see his father dead so he could ascend to the throne. In contrast, David told his generals, **"Be gentle with the young man Absalom for my sake"** (2 Samuel 18:5).

The battle took place in the Forest of Ephraim with Absalom's army being defeated by David's men. It was a fierce battle with 20,000 casualties. As Absalom retreated with his army, the mule he was riding went under a large oak tree with low-hanging branches.

Absalom was known to have long, thick hair. It got tangled in the tree. His mule kept going, leaving Absalom hanging in midair.

One of David's soldiers saw Absalom hanging in the oak tree and reported this to Joab. Joab was incredulous that the soldier hadn't kill him. But the soldier reminded Joab about King David's instructions not to harm Absalom. Joab didn't care. He took three javelins and went and found Absalom. Joab plunged all three javelins into Absalom's heart. He then had his men take the king's son down and dig a pit in the forest. Joab buried his cousin Absalom under a pile of rocks. Joab directly disobeyed his king and, in doing so, murdered Absalom.

When David learned that Absalom had been killed, grief overwhelmed him: **"O my son Absalom! My son, my son Absalom! If only I had died instead of you—O Absalom, my son, my son!"** (1 Samuel 18:33).

And David mourned the death of Absalom.

Because Joab had willfully disobeyed the king's order, David demoted Joab and relieved him of his rank as commander of the army. In Joab's place, David appointed another one of his nephews, a man by the name of Amasa. As a nephew, Amasa was also Joab's cousin. Nepotism was pretty common in the ancient world.

David returned to his palace in Jerusalem, but his troubles weren't over. Another rebel named Sheba led the northern parts of Israel to revolt against David as king: **"We have no share in David, no part in Jesse's** son! Every man to his tent, Israel!" (2 Samuel 20:1). So David summoned his army to pursue Sheba immediately to put down the rebellion. The army headed north and arrived in Gibeon. Recall earlier, it was at Gibeon where Ish-Bosheth's army, under the command of Abner, had been routed by David's army.

On this occasion, Joab approached Amasa, his commander, as to welcome him with a brotherly kiss:

> **Joab said to Amasa, "How are you, my brother?" Then Joab took Amasa by the beard with his right hand to kiss him. Amasa was not on his guard against the dagger in Joab's hand, and Joab plunged it into his belly, and his intestines spilled out on the ground. Without being stabbed again, Amasa died.** (2 Samuel 20:9,10)

And David mourned the death of Amasa.

There is one more story of treachery we need to look at from when King David was nearing the end of his life. David had another son by the name of Adonijah. Adonijah was David's fourth son, born shortly after Absalom. One day Adonijah decided that he wanted to be king, even though his father was still alive. Adonijah conferred with Joab and with Abiathar the priest. Abiathar was one of the priests whom the double agent Hushai sent to warn David about Absalom's battle strategy. Joab and Abiathar supported the would-be king, Adonijah.

When word about Adonijah's self-made kingship reached those loyal to David, they acted decisively. David had decades earlier promised to Bathsheba that their son Solomon would succeed David as king. David immediately gave the order that Solomon should be anointed as king. Solomon was taken to Gihon where Zadok the priest and Nathan the prophet anointed him as king.

When Adonijah and his supporters heard that David anointed Solomon as the next king, they all fled. Adonijah fled to the temple and appealed for clemency by taking hold of the altar. Solomon allowed his half brother Adonijah to live as long as he made no further trouble. But Adonijah did not stop scheming. In the end, Solomon had Adonijah executed along with Joab because he had murdered two of David's commanders, Abner and Amasa, during peacetime. He also removed Abiathar as priest for his role in Adonijah's coup attempt.

What a tragic story of treachery—murder, rape, another murder, a suicide, and another two murders—all transpiring from David's original crimes of adultery and murder.

Our takeaway from David's family is sadly clear. Sin has consequences, even for a man after God's own heart.

David set a terrible example for his family when he betrayed one of his mighty men, Uriah, by sleeping with his wife and having him killed in a cover-up scheme. Did the members of David's family think his actions gave them a license to commit crimes of their own? It appears so. Not only did David's crimes set a terrible example; David also found it difficult to hold others accountable for their criminal activity.

We ought never to take sin lightly because it can have repercussions for generations to come. Our personal sin needs to be confessed, repented of, and forgiven. Our gracious God wants us to do this because of what his Son, Jesus, did for us.

EHUD

So far we've considered the crimes of Cain, Moses, King David, and King David's family. For the next few chapters, we'll focus on the period of the judges detailed in the Old Testament book by the same name.

The book of Judges sketches out the history of God's chosen people, the Israelites, after they took possession of the Promised Land, which is also known as the land of Canaan. Israel's leader at that time was Joshua, who succeeded Moses. The time from Joshua's death until the time of Samuel the prophet is known as the "period of the judges." Samuel, by the way, was the prophet during the reigns of King Saul and King David. In terms of history, the period of the judges extended from about 1350 B.C. to about 1050 B.C., approximately three hundred years. I should also mention that Bible scholars don't always agree on dates and time frames, including these dates. So just think of the period of the judges as being from the time of Joshua until the time of the prophet Samuel.

During these three centuries, there were no royal rulers in Israel. Based upon the covenant that the Lord gave to Moses on Mt. Sinai and reaffirmed with Joshua, every tribe, clan, and family was to be responsible for remaining faithful to the Lord's covenant. Every Israelite pledged allegiance to the Lord and to the nation when they went to the tabernacle for designated feasts and sacrifices.

During the period of the judges, the tabernacle was located in the town of Shiloh. Shiloh was somewhat centrally located among the 12 tribes, a town located in the hill country of the tribe of Ephraim. The tabernacle remained in Shiloh throughout the period of the judges.

Sadly, as the book of Judges reveals, God's Old Testament people were not faithful to the Lord or his covenant. Time and time again, the nation abandoned the worship of the Lord in order to chase after other gods. The last verse in the book of Judges sums up the spirit of the times: **"In those days Israel had no king; everyone did as they saw fit"** (21:25).

The book of Judges is a collection of short stories. It begins with an account chronicling how successful *and* yet unsuccessful the 12 tribes were at taking possession of the Promised Land. Although the Lord wanted his people to take full possession of the land previously occupied by the Canaanite people, they didn't always accomplish what the Lord had instructed them to do. They allowed foreigners to live among them instead of driving them out. This would cause them problems in the years and decades to come.

After this opening historical recap, we next read

about the individual stories of 12 judges. Maybe this is a good place to pause and make a comment about the word *judges*. When you think of a judge, what comes to mind? The most common English usage of the noun *judge* is someone who administers justice in a court of law. But the Old Testament judges didn't wear black robes, nor did they sit in courtrooms. But they did administer justice, the Lord's justice. They were leaders of the people and sometimes described as deliverers or warriors. They were each called by the Lord to deliver the nation of Israel from the hand of a foreign oppressor. The oppressors were from various nations that bordered the land of Israel.

In the book of Judges, we see a pattern, or a historical cycle, that developed in the nation of Israel over the course of decades. In the book of Judges, there are seven of these cycles in which the 12 judges served.

What did this pattern or cycle look like? There were four phases in each of these cycles. First, there was REST. For example, after Joshua led the 12 tribes to take possession of the Promised Land, there was a period of rest and peace. But after Joshua died, the people started to backslide spiritually. They turned away from the Lord and turned toward the countless idols of the nations around them. This happened frequently because the people of Israel intermarried with the idol-worshiping peoples whom they did not drive out from the Promised Land.

This second phase in the cycle was REBELLION. The rebellion phase is most often described as "the

Israelites did evil in the eyes of the LORD."

Because of Israel's rebellion, the Lord then allowed a neighboring nation to oppress the Israelites and RULE over them, sometimes for years and even decades. After this foreign oppression and rule, eventually the people would cry out to the Lord for deliverance. The Lord would hear their cries and then would send a RESCUER, a deliverer, a judge.

The four phases in each of these cycles were REST when there was a strong leader, REBELLION against the Lord after the leader died, then oppression and RULE by a nearby nation. And then RESCUE by a judge. REST, REBELLION, RULE, and RESCUE. It's a pattern repeated in each of the seven cycles.

The first judge was a man by the name of Othniel. While Joshua was alive, Israel enjoyed a period of rest and peace. But when Joshua died, the people rebelled against the Lord and did evil in his eyes by worshiping the Baals and the Asherahs. Baal was the Canaanite god of rain, wind, and fertility. Because the land of Canaan, which the Israelites now occupied, depended on rain to grow crops, Baal was the top dog (dog is god—little g—spelled backward) among the Canaanite people. Asherah was another popular deity in Canaan. She was the goddess of motherhood and fertility. Asherah was either Baal's mother, his lover, or both. The two of them would mate with the result that the rainy season would come and bring an end to the dry season.

So why in the world would the Israelites be constantly

tempted to worship Baal and Asherah? Well, one of the most common rituals in worshiping Baal and Asherah was to have sex with temple prostitutes. These immoral activities were meant to inspire Baal and Asherah to do their thing so they would provide rain. There was more to the worship of Baal than just the sexual aspects. It also included black magic and even child sacrifice. Needless to say, all these aspects of idol worship were evil in the eyes of the Lord.

Because of this idol worship, the Lord gave the Israelites into the hands of Cushan-Rishathaim, king of Aram, a nation to the northeast of Israel, also known as the nation of Syria. The Israelites were subject to the rule of Cushan for eight years. As the years went along, the people cried out to the Lord, so the Lord sent Othniel to go to war against Cushan. Othniel defeated him and rescued Israel.

What followed was 40 years of rest and peace for the land of Israel until Othniel died. The Hebrew word for "peace" that is used here is not the familiar *Shalom*, which was used as a greeting or blessing. The word for "peace" here means "an absence of war." For 40 years there was no war in Israel. The first of the seven cycles was complete.

Which finally brings us to the judge I want to talk about in this chapter—a man by the name of Ehud. He is known for assassinating a king. Ehud was the second of the 12 judges.

After Othniel died, the book of Judges tells us,

"Again the Israelites did evil in the eyes of the Lord, and because they did this evil the Lord gave Eglon king of Moab power over Israel" (Judges 3:12). The period of rest and peace came to an end because the Israelites did evil in the eyes of the Lord. We're not told specifically what that evil was, but undoubtedly it was idolatry. Eglon, king of Moab, rose to power. And why? Because the Lord gave power to him. Keep that in mind for later.

King Eglon formed a coalition against Israel. He recruited the Ammonites, who lived east of Israel, and the Amalekites, who lived south of Israel, to join him.

Eglon's coalition attacked Israel and took possession of the City of Palms, which was also known as Jericho, located about five miles west of the Jordan River. Then for 18 years, King Eglon demanded tribute money from the Israelites. **"Again the Israelites cried out to the Lord, and he gave them a deliverer—Ehud, a left-handed man, the son of Gera the Benjamite. The Israelites sent [Ehud] with tribute to Eglon king of Moab"** (Judges 3:15).

Ehud was the Lord's appointed rescuer for Israel. We're told two things about him. He was left-handed and from the tribe of Benjamin. Do you know what the name Benjamin means in Hebrew? It means "son of the right hand." So we've got a left-handed man from the tribe of Benjamin whose name means the "son of the right hand." Interesting, don't you think? What's up with this detail about Ehud being left-handed?

Here are two possibilities. One is that Ehud was a

natural lefty. Natural lefties are historically in the minority, no matter what the culture or time. Some say they comprise between 5 percent and 30 percent of any nation or culture. The other possibility was that he had a physical abnormality with his right hand. You see, the Hebrew expression for left-handedness means "restricted as to the right hand." Ehud could have had some sort of right-handed restriction. When I was a kid, I had a shirttail relative, about my age, who was born with one shortened arm and with no hand. Could that have been similar to Ehud's condition? I don't know for sure, but it's a possibility. I'm inclined to think that Ehud wasn't a natural lefty because of the events that followed.

We're told that Ehud made himself a small double-edged sword, the length of which was a measurement from the elbow to the clenched knuckles of a man's hand. He strapped this sword to his right thigh. For the average person, this would be a sword 16-18 inches in length. I'm above average in height, but even so, if I strapped a 16-inch sword to my right thigh, it would definitely extend past my knee. So did Ehud strap this to his right thigh both above and below the knee so that he wasn't able to bend his right knee, forcing him to walk with a limp?

I think about these questions because why in the world would King Eglon's bodyguards not do a body search of Ehud before he was allowed in the same room as the king? Did Ehud approach the throne room as a man who was crippled in his right hand and walking with a limp, suggesting he couldn't possibly be a threat to the king? Or did the guards do a body search of Ehud only on the left side where most men, who were right-handed, would carry a weapon? The Bible doesn't tell us, but I'm inclined to think of Ehud planning this ruse of being a weakling with the hope that his murderous intentions wouldn't be found out.

At any rate, Ehud entered the king's palace with the tribute carried by some other men. Ehud presented the tribute to King Eglon, who was described as a very fat man, excessively obese. After presenting the tribute, Ehud dismissed the men who had carried in the tribute. Apparently, Ehud went with them until they reached Gilgal, which was only a mile or so north of Jericho. At Gilgal, Ehud turned around and went back to the king with the message: **"Your Majesty, I have a secret message for you"** (Judges 3:19). It was a *secret* message.

King Eglon was intrigued by what Ehud had to offer. He was eager to hear this *secret* message. So the king sent everyone out of the upper room of his summer palace so that only he and Ehud remained. Ehud said, **"'I have a message from God for you.' As the king rose from his seat, Ehud reached with his left hand, drew the sword from his right thigh and plunged it into the king's belly"** (Judges 3:20,21). Now this is where the details of this assassination get a little graphic: **"Even the handle sank in after the blade, and his bowels discharged. Ehud did not pull the sword out, and the fat** closed in over it" (Judges 3:22). This could be a made-for-Netflix movie!

Ehud escaped the upper room by going out on the porch, but not before locking the doors to the upper room. When Eglon's servants later found the king dead, Ehud had already escaped. Ehud headed to the town of Seirah, located in the hill country of the tribe of Ephraim. There Ehud blew a ram's horn to rally the people of his own tribe, the tribe of Benjamin, as well as the people from the tribe of Ephraim.

The lands of Ephraim and Benjamin shared a border. Ehud told the people, **"Follow me . . . for the Lord has given Moab, your enemy, into your hands"** (Judges 3:28). Ehud and the Israelites headed east and took possession of the fords of the Jordan River that led to Moab. The fords of the Jordan were places in the river that were shallow and allowed people to cross easily. The Israelites didn't allow any of the Moabites to cross over, killing about 10,000 Moabites, all described in our English translations as "vigorous and strong." But the Hebrew has a different shade of meaning, "strong and well-rounded," like their king was well-rounded. **"That day Moab was made subject to Israel, and the land had peace for eighty years"** (Judges 3:30). It was the longest peaceful time recorded during the time of the judges.

Now I wouldn't be surprised if you're questioning whether or not Ehud actually committed a crime. After all, Ehud was called by the Lord to rescue Israel from their enemies, the Moabites. As did Othniel, Ehud could have assembled an army and attacked the Moabites at Jericho. Instead, he risked his own life to end the life of the king of Moab. So was Ehud's assassination of King Eglon a crime?

It was most certainly a crime, a capital offense, from the perspective of the Moabites. But we can also make the case that it wasn't a crime from the perspective of the Lord, who sanctioned it for the rescuing of his chosen people. This event reminds us that not all things are black and white in the Bible.

This account is a rather graphic scene in the Bible, but it is also quite insightful. There are a couple of takeaways for us. First and foremost, this is a story about the Lord's love for his people. The Israelites certainly didn't deserve the Lord's love because they were doing what was evil in his eyes. They worshiped the Baals and the Asherahs instead of the Lord. In love God had an enemy of his people oppress Israel and rule over them for 18 years. And why? To lead the nation of Israel to repent, which they did. It should be no surprise to us that God allows things to happen to lead people and even entire nations to repent and turn back to him.

Second, we see how the Lord used just one man to change the course of a nation in a single day—an entire nation's future changed in a single day. That's the power of the God of heaven and earth. That's the power of the God we worship and serve. The story of Ehud is the story of God's love and God's power.

JAEL

The crime we're going to investigate in this chapter took place in Israel during the time of Judge Deborah. Deborah was not only a judge in Israel, but she was also a prophet. Judges chapter 4 begins with the pattern that I mentioned last chapter:

> **Again the Israelites did evil in the eyes of the Lord, now that Ehud was dead. So the Lord sold them into the hands of Jabin king of Canaan, who reigned in Hazor. Sisera, the commander of his army, was based in Harosheth Haggoyim. Because he had nine hundred chariots fitted with iron and had cruelly oppressed the Israelites for twenty years, they** [the people] **cried to the Lord for help."** (verses 1-3)

We've got a bunch of names and places to sort out here. Let's start with the city of Hazor. Hazor was a strategically located city about ten miles north of the Sea of Galilee. It was a mountainous region on a major trade route in ancient times. We first hear about Hazor during the time of Joshua as he was leading Israel to conquer the land of Canaan. Joshua chapter 11 tells us that Joshua won a great battle at Hazor against a king named Jabin. Jabin led an alliance of Canaanite cities.

Already at the time of Joshua, King Jabin had chariots in his army. With this victory over Jabin, Joshua burned the city to the ground. The Canaanite people would rebuild the city. And at the time of Deborah, which was a century and a half later, another king named Jabin ruled this city and the surrounding area.

Two other details about Hazor are worth mentioning. During the reign of King Solomon, he had the city of Hazor fortified to defend the northern border from any threats from Syria and Assyria. When the Assyrian king, Tiglath-Pileser, invaded the land of Israel two hundred years after Solomon lived, Hazor was one of the first cities captured. Its residents were deported into Assyria. The other detail about Hazor is a contemporary one. Today Hazor is the largest archaeological site in Israel.

So Jabin was the king of Hazor. Sisera was his general. We're told that Sisera lived in Harosheth Haggoyim. This probably wasn't the name of a city or town. The phrase means "metal forge of the foreign nations." It was likely the name of Sisera's military base where he had a weapons factory that manufactured iron chariots.

Chariots were the tanks of the ancient world. Each chariot had two wheels and was pulled by a horse. They could maneuver easily and tear through a battle line of soldiers on foot. Sisera had nine hundred of these iron chariots at his disposal. And it was to King Jabin that the Lord sold the people of Israel because they, once again, had done evil in the eyes of the Lord.

We're not told specifically what the evil was that Israel did, simply that they once again did evil. We do get a sense, however, of what this evil was in the next chapter where Deborah recounted Israel's recent history. She said, **"Villagers in Israel would not fight; they held back until I, Deborah, arose, until I arose, a mother in Israel. God chose new leaders when war came to the city gates, but not a shield or spear was seen among forty thousand in Israel"** (Judges 5:7,8). This suggests that the people had lost their will to fight for the Lord's land and instead chose to worship the gods of the Canaanite people. And remember the worship of Baal and Asherah involved sexual activity with the temple prostitutes. The attitude in Israel could be summed up with the 1960s Vietnam-era expression, "Make love, not war."

As a result of this evil, the Lord allowed Jabin's army under the command of Sisera to oppress the people of Israel. It was a cruel oppression. The Hebrew word has the meaning of violence. This oppression lasted for two decades, during which time the people once again cried out to the Lord for deliverance.

Let's learn a little bit about Deborah. Here is what Judges chapter 4 says about her: **"Deborah, a prophet, the wife of Lappidoth, was leading Israel at that time. She held court under the Palm of Deborah between**

Ramah and Bethel in the hill country of Ephraim, and the Israelites went up to her to have their disputes decided" (verses 4,5).

In these two sentences, there is once again a lot to unpack. First, the name Deborah. In Hebrew, it is the name for a bee, like a honeybee. Deborah was married to a man named Lappidoth. Deborah was also a prophetess. Both male and female prophets in the Old Testament were mouthpieces of the Lord. They spoke the word of the Lord. Unlike a warrior judge like Ehud, Deborah was also a judge like we think of a judge. She held court publicly under the Palm of Deborah between Ramah and Bethel. Ramah and Bethel were about five miles apart in the hill country near the border of the tribe of Benjamin and the tribe of Ephraim.

It would be reasonable to conclude that the Palm of Deborah was named after Deborah the prophetess and judge. But it's also possible that this was a different Deborah who lived at the time of Isaac and Rebekah. Rebekah had a nurse named Deborah who died and was buried under an oak tree just south of Bethel. This is the same area where Deborah was holding court. Some Bible scholars wonder if this oak tree under which nurse Deborah was buried and the Palm of Deborah are one in the same. Interesting possibility, but we just don't know for sure.

From her court under the Palm of Deborah, Deborah sent for Barak. Barak was a mighty warrior and commander of the army. The name Barak means "lightning." When Barak arrived, Deborah told him: "The LORD, the God of Israel, commands you: 'Go, take with you ten thousand men of Naphtali and Zebulun and lead the way to Mount Tabor. I will lead Sisera, the commander of Jabin's army, with his chariots and his troops to the Kishon River and give them into your hands'" (Judges 4:6,7). Deborah delivered the Lord's message that told Barak that he would be able to defeat Sisera's army, even with his nine hundred chariots, because the Lord was with Barak and Israel. The Lord promised victory.

Barak hesitated. Maybe he was thinking about Sisera's nine hundred deadly iron chariots. *"We have zero, zilch, nada. How could we ever possibly defeat them?"* I get it, and I'd probably hesitate too. What about you? Barak hesitated, revealing a lack of faith and trust in the promises of God. Barak said to Deborah, **"If you go with me, I will go; but if you don't go with me, I won't go"** (Judges 4:8). Deborah agreed to go, but because of Barak's lack of faith in God, she told him that the credit for the victory would not go to him but to a woman. Deborah went with Barak to Kedesh and there assembled a 10,000-strong army.

If you read Judges chapter 4, what you're told next seems irrelevant to the story line: **"Now Heber the Kenite had left the other Kenites, the descendants of Hobab, Moses' brother-in-law, and pitched his tent by the great tree in Zaanannim near Kedesh"** (verse 11). So what does Heber have to do with this? And who is he? Hang on; you'll find out in just a bit.

Barak and his men marched up Mt. Tabor. When Sisera learned that Barak was on Mt. Tabor, he gathered his iron chariots and all the men with him and headed to the Kishon River, which was just a small stream during the dry season. Then Deborah said to Barak: **"Go! This is the day the Lord has given Sisera into your hands. Has not the Lord gone ahead of you?"** (verse 14).

What does it mean: "Has not the Lord gone ahead of you"? Hang on; I'll get to that too. Barak came down the mountain with his 10,000 soldiers and routed Sisera and his iron chariots. Does it seem like some details are missing? They are. The details of this battle are in Judges chapter 5, included in what's known as the Song of Deborah.

The phrase "has not the Lord gone ahead of you" referred to something only the Lord could do. Deborah tells us in her victory song: **"The earth shook, the heavens poured, the clouds poured down water. The river Kishon swept them away, the age-old river, the river Kishon"** (Judges 5:4,21). The Lord had sent a massive rainstorm. The ground turned to mud, bogging down Sisera's chariots. What had been a trickling stream had become a roaring river, sweeping many of Sisera's soldiers away. Barak and his men pursued Sisera's army, and not a one of Israel's enemies survived, except for Sisera.

Sisera got off his chariot that was stuck in the mud and fled to the tent of Yael (in English we would say

Jael). Jael was the wife of Heber the Kenite. Remember the reference that seemed to be inserted into the story? Well, now you know why.

But there's more. Sisera fled to the tent of Jael and Heber **"because there was an alliance between Jabin king of Hazor and the family of Heber the Kenite** (Judges 4:17). There was some kind of peace treaty between Jabin and the Kenites, and Sisera knew it. With such a peace treaty came a highly respected code of hospitality, which was practiced all across the Middle East. When Jael went out to meet Sisera to invite him into her tent, she was guaranteeing Sisera's health and safety.

Jael invited the exhausted Sisera into her tent, had him lie down on a mat, and covered him with a blanket. When he asked for a drink of water, Jael instead gave him warm milk to drink. After he fell asleep, Jael ignored the code of hospitality between King Jabin and her husband, Heber. She picked up a tent stake and hammer and drove the stake through Sisera's temple and into the ground.

Barak was in pursuit of Sisera. When he came near Jael's tent, she went out of her tent and told Barak that she could show him the man he was looking for. And she did. Victory was secured on this day by Jael, not Barak. This was the first of more battles to come against King Jabin, but eventually Israel was victorious and there was peace—no war—for the next 40 years.

So was what Jael did to Sisera a crime of murder? It certainly wasn't self-defense. Jael was a civilian, not a soldier, so this can't be considered a battlefield death. And what Jael did went against everything she knew about practicing hospitality with an ally. So what do you think?

In the last chapter, we talked about different perspectives. What Jael did was a crime of murder from King Jabin's perspective. He lost the commander of his army. What Jael did was a crime of murder from the perspective of Sisera's mother. At the end of the Song of Deborah, there is a caricature of Sisera's mother. Listen how she is described: **"Through the window peered Sisera's mother; behind the lattice she cried out, 'Why is his chariot so long in coming? Why is the clatter of his chariot delayed?' The wisest of her ladies answer her; indeed, she keeps saying to herself, 'Are they not finding and dividing the spoils: a woman or two for each man, colorful garments as plunder for Sisera, colorful garments embroidered, highly embroidered garments for my neck—all this as plunder?'"** (Judges 5:28-30).

From the perspective of the rulers and people of Hazor, this was murder.

But not from the Lord's perspective. King Jabin and the people of Hazor were enemies of God's people. The Lord, through Deborah, indicated the *glory* of defeating Sisera and his army would go to a woman. Between the Lord sending the downpour of rain to make nine hundred iron chariots useless to Jael's tent-pegging Sisera's head, this was the Lord's plan to rescue his people from their enemies.

Is there anything we can learn from the story of Deborah, Barak, and Jael? I think so. The Lord called Deborah to serve as Israel's only female judge and to be his mouthpiece as a prophetess. What stands out for me is that Deborah was a great encourager to Barak as she demonstrated her faith in the words and promises of the Lord. She's a woman worth emulating!

Then there is Barak, who hesitated, who initially lacked faith in the words and promises of the Lord. Yet in the end, his weakness was turned into strength. It took great courage to come charging down Mt. Tabor to face nine hundred iron chariots. Did you know that Barak is mentioned in Hebrews chapter 11, standing with other great people of faith?

The final takeaway is that those who do not remain faithful to the Lord God lose out on his blessing. It is only through repentance that we can enjoy all that the Lord wants to give us. This was a truth that Old Testament Israel struggled to learn throughout its history. We can do better.

I think the last stanza in the Song of Deborah makes the contrast between the Lord's enemies and those faithful to him crystal clear. Deborah sang these words: **"So may all your enemies perish, Lord! But may they who love you be like the sun when it rises in its strength"** (Judges 5:31).

THE LEVITE AND HIS CONCUBINE

Just so you know, the crimes that we are investigating in this chapter are some of the most shocking and appalling crimes in the entire Bible, so be prepared. We're going to answer two questions: *Why is this even in the Bible?* and *What can we learn from it?* Here's a clue—we learn a lot about what happened during the period of the judges and how it relates to what's going on in our culture today.

Following the Bible's account of Deborah, we learn about more judges whom the Lord sent to rescue Israel, rescuers such as Gibeon, Jephthah, Samson, and others less well known. But after Samson died, detailed in Judges chapter 16, there are no further judges mentioned in this book of the Bible, yet there are five more chapters in the book of Judges.

These chapters detail short stories of what was typical in the families, in the tribes, among the Levite religious leaders, and with the nation as a whole during the period of judges. The phrase "In those days Israel had no king" occurs four times in these five chapters. Two times, in both the first and last occurrences, there is an additional phrase: "Everyone did as they saw fit."

The crimes we are investigating here involve a religious leader, an old man, and two women. The sordid details are recorded in the last three chapters of the book of Judges. The crime of the religious leader and the old man is appalling. What followed among the men of a town in Israel is pure evil. How the religious leader responded to that evil led to a politically charged inferno that spread across the entire nation. It almost led to the genocide of an entire tribe in Israel. "In those days Israel had no king; everyone did as they saw fit."

Chapter 19 begins by telling us about a nameless Levite, a religious leader, who lived in a remote area of Ephraim. The fact that this Levite lived in a remote area is significant. When Israel conquered the land of Canaan, 11 of the tribes received a geographical area as their own. But the descendants of Levi, who served as priests and other religious leaders, were assigned to 48 different *cities* throughout Israel. This Levite should have been living in one of these 48 cities, not out in the boonies.

The Levite took a concubine from a family in Bethlehem, located in the tribe of Judah. A concubine was a woman who lived with a man but had a lower status than a wife. Why the difference? Some scholars suggest that a wife brought a dowry to a marriage relationship, but a concubine didn't. A concubine relationship could also be entered into without the formal ceremonies of marriage as prescribed by the culture. It was a legitimate marriage. A concubine could not leave the marriage or go back to her parent's home.

The Levite's concubine, also nameless, was unfaithful to the Levite. The Hebrew language suggests the unfaithfulness was of a sexual nature. Did she have an affair? Did she engage in prostitution for money? We don't know. We do know that she chose to leave the Levite and return to her father's house in Bethlehem. After four months, the Levite traveled to Bethlehem to persuade his concubine to come back home.

When he arrived, his concubine brought him into her father's house. The Levite's father-in-law gladly welcomed him, not something we might expect. The father-in-law convinced the Levite to stay a couple of days, which turned into three, then four. Finally, on the afternoon of the fifth day, the Levite told his concubine, "We gotta go." So the Levite, his concubine, and his servant left Bethlehem and headed north.

Later in the afternoon, they approached the city of Jebus, which would later be known as Jerusalem. From Bethlehem to Jerusalem was about five miles. The servant suggested they stop and spend the night. The Levite refused. Jebus was inhabited by Jebusites, not Israelites. So they continued on to the town of Gibeah, which was another six or seven miles north of Jebus. Note for now that Gibeah was a town in the tribe of Benjamin. That's significant. They entered Gibeah and went to the city square.

Do you recall the law of hospitality from the story about Jael? General Sisera was welcomed into Heber and Jael's tent because they shared a treaty. In ancient cultures, that meant that Jael was guaranteeing Sisera's safety and well-being. We also saw how Jael set aside that law of hospitality to carry out the Lord's plan to save his people. That law of hospitality applied also to visitors who came into a city square. Town residents were to take traveling visitors into their homes and offer them food, shelter, and even feed their animals.

An old man came into the town square from working out in the fields. He asked the Levite where he was from. When the old man learned that the Levite was from his own hometown area in the hill country of Ephraim, he invited the Levite and his companions to his home. Initially, the Levite indicated they would just stay in the town square, but the old man convinced them to come to his house. The old man fed the donkeys, washed the feet of his visitors, and gave them something to eat and drink. The law of hospitality was at work.

But then something tragic happened. A group of men from Gibeah, described as "wicked men," came pounding on the old man's front door. They wanted the old man to send out the Levite so they could really get to know his houseguest, which was another way of saying, "We want to use him for our sexual pleasure." Here's the Bible's account of this exchange:

> **The owner of the house went outside and**

said to them, "No, my friends, don't be so vile. Since this man is my guest, don't do this outrageous thing. Look, here is my virgin daughter, and his concubine. I will bring them out to you now, and you can use them and do to them whatever you wish. But as for this man, don't do such an outrageous thing."

But the men would not listen to him. So the man [the Levite] **took his concubine and sent her outside to them, and they raped her and abused her throughout the night, and at dawn they let her go. At daybreak the woman went back to the house where her master was staying, fell down at the door and lay there until daylight.** (Judges 19:23-26)

The old man correctly stated that men having sex with men was a vile and evil thing. But then he went on to offer these local monsters his own virgin daughter and the concubine of his guest!? That wouldn't be vile as well? Apparently, the sexual violation of women was less shameful than that of men, at least from a male perspective.

What's worse is that the Levite, a religious leader in Israel, sent his concubine—whom he had just traveled to Bethlehem to convince to come back home—out the door of the old man's home for the mob to do with as they wanted. Appalling, to say the least. By morning, the concubine had crawled back to the doorstep of the old man's home. When the Levite opened the door in the morning, he found his concubine unresponsive.

Does this event remind you of anything? How about the day that two angels, who took on the appearance of men, went to the city of Sodom, where Abraham's nephew Lot lived with his family. Lot met these two angel men at the city gate and invited them to his home. Initially, the two angels said they would just stay in the town square, but eventually Lot persuaded them to stay at his home.

That evening a group of men, both young and old, came to Lot's house demanding that he send out his two guests so they, again, could get to know them better. Lot went out of his house and refused their request, again in keeping with the law of hospitality. Sadly, Lot offered his two daughters to the group of men instead.

What's different in the two accounts is that the angels pulled Lot back into the house. When the mob was about to break down the door, the angels blinded the group of men so they couldn't find the door. Although Lot was willing to give his two daughters to the mob, his daughters were spared by the angels' action.

The point of the story of the old man and the Levite and the men of Gibeah is that Israel, during the time of the judges, had become Sodom and Gomorrah. In Israel, during the period of the judges, there was a culture of lawlessness, violence, and death. As this story demonstrates, this culture of violence and death was even found among the religious leaders of the day. That's the reason this story, appalling as it is, is in the Bible. It demonstrates that when people walk away from being obedient to the Lord God, evil will soon dominate their lives and their culture, even among religious leaders. There is more evil to come in this story . . .

When the Levite opened the door of the old man's house and found his concubine unresponsive, he put her on his donkey and headed home to the hill country of Ephraim. If the concubine wasn't already dead on the doorstep of the old man's home, she would be by the time the Levite got home. Again from the biblical text: **"When he reached home, he took a knife and cut up his concubine, limb by limb, into twelve parts and sent them into all the areas of Israel. Everyone who saw was saying to one another, 'Such a thing has never been seen or done, not since the day the Israelites came up out of Egypt'"** (Judges 19:29,30).

The Levite butchered his concubine and sent her body parts throughout the land. It was done to create a reaction, and it got a reaction. People throughout Israel were shocked and appalled. Nothing like this had ever been done before.

But what the Levite did also demonstrated how callous and wicked the nation had become, including the Levite himself. In Israel, as well as throughout the Middle East, the proper burial of a deceased person was a spiritual norm. According to the Lord's law given on Mt. Sinai, the people of Israel were required to bury even the dead bodies of criminals. The way the Levite treated the body of his concubine showed shameless disregard for the law of the Lord.

The result of the Levite's ghoulish gifts to the tribes of Israel was that representatives from all the tribes, except Benjamin, gathered to determine what they should do. This gathering took place at Mizpah, a town located about five miles north of Gibeah. At this gathering, the tribal representatives wanted to know how this awful thing happened.

So the Levite testified. As you read these verses, ask yourself, what didn't he say or what should he have said?

> **I and my concubine came to Gibeah in Benjamin to spend the night. During the night the men of Gibeah came after me and surrounded the house, intending to kill me. They raped my concubine, and she died. I took my concubine, cut her into pieces and sent one piece to each region of Israel's inheritance, because they committed this lewd and outrageous act in Israel.** (Judges 20:4-6)

What's your reaction to the Levite's testimony? I think he shared the basic facts of what happened but did so in a misleading and selective way. What didn't he say? He didn't mention that the old man, in a self-serving manner, had offered up his own virgin daughter as well as the Levite's concubine. The Levite didn't mention that he had pushed his own concubine out of the house to be used and abused by these men. The Levite took no responsibility for what had happened. There was no confession of what he had done or not done. He correctly identified the wrong done by the men of Gibeah but took no accountability for his own actions. It was another example of the Levite, a religious leader, being morally bankrupt.

Upon hearing the Levite's testimony, the representatives at the Mizpah assembly unanimously decided that the men who raped and murdered the concubine needed to be put to death. That would be justice. The representatives also took an oath at Mizpah: **"Not one of us will give his daughter in marriage to a Benjamite"** (Judges 21:1).

The coalition of the 11 tribes put together a fighting force of 400,000 men. The coalition sent men among the people of Benjamin to turn over the guilty parties. The tribe of Benjamin chose to defend the men of Gibeah. They showed their hand by raising a rebel force of 26,000 to defend Gibeah. According to Judges 20:16, there were 700 select soldiers among them who were left-handed, each of whom could sling a stone with amazing accuracy.

What happened next is the only bright spot in this sordid story. When the tribe of Benjamin refused to allow justice to be served, the coalition traveled to Bethel, only a few miles away, to inquire of the Lord what they should do. There the leaders inquired of the

Lord: **"'Who of us is to go up first to fight against the Benjamites?' The** Lord **replied, 'Judah shall go first'"** (Judges 20:18). The next morning, the coalition headed to Gibeah. On this first day of battle, the coalition suffered heavy losses, 22,000 soldiers.

Because of their losses, the leaders inquired of the Lord a second time whether they should go to battle against their brothers. The Lord said yes. On the second day of battle, the coalition's losses were almost as great; 18,000 were killed. So what was going on here? The Lord told them to go into battle, and they lost 40,000 men in two days. Why? Recall when the coalition went throughout the people of Benjamin demanding the men of Gibeah. What they led with in those conversations was, "How could you Benjamin people let this happen?" It revealed a self-righteous, moral superiority. The Lord had a lesson to teach them.

For a third time the leaders asked the Lord if they should continue the fight. This time they fasted and made two offerings to the Lord, a burnt offering and a fellowship offering that signified their dependence on the Lord. The coalition repented of their arrogance and smugness and put their trust in the Lord. The Lord's response this time was, **"Go, for tomorrow I will give them into your hands"** (Judges 20:28).

On the third day of battle, the coalition set an ambush all around Gibeah. One force attacked Gibeah as they had the previous two days and drew out the Benjamites from the city. The Benjamite forces were beginning to have success again, but then the coalition forces retreated with the Benjamite army in hot pursuit. While this battle was going on, the ambush of the city took place by 10,000 crack coalition forces. They set fire to the city.

When the Benjamites saw the smoke, they returned to Gibeah but were caught in between two coalition forces. The coalition forces were victorious, and 25,000 Benjamite soldiers were killed. Only 600 survived by fleeing into the desert. The coalition then went throughout the tribe of Benjamin, burning every city and killing all the women, children, and even animals. The ruthlessness of the coalition forces against Benjamin was devastating. Just think about this . . . the rape and murder of 1 concubine led to the deaths of 65,000 Israelite soldiers plus all the women and children of Benjamin.

After the slaughter of the people of Benjamin, the coalition leaders essentially asked themselves, "What have we done?" With no women left in Benjamin and the fact that all 11 tribes swore an oath at Mizpah that they would never give a daughter in marriage to a man from Benjamin, what would they do to prevent the tribe of Benjamin from becoming extinct? Here's what they did.

There was one city in Israel that had not sent a representative to the gathering in Mizpah. It was the city of Jabesh Gilead located on the east side of the Jordan River. Nor did they send any men to fight in the coalition army. Their nonparticipation said two things. They gave unspoken approval to what the men of Gibeah had done, and they didn't value solidarity with the rest of Israel. Both of these were capital offenses. So the coalition sent 12,000 fighting men to Jabesh Gilead. Everyone in the city was to be put to death except for women who were virgins. Four hundred women who had never slept with a man were brought back to become the wives of the 600 Benjamin men who had survived.

But they were still 200 women short.

Another plan. There was a religious festival that Israel celebrated each year. It was held at Shiloh where the tabernacle was. It was likely the Feast of Tabernacles in the fall of the year. The leaders told the remaining 200 Benjamin males to go to the festival and abduct the young women who would be dancing at the festival. Each was to abduct one of them and take her home to be his wife. Problem solved.

After hearing this account, don't you just want to scream at the immorality, the inequality, the selective morality, the unethical approach to solving problems, the rape and murder, the selfishness, the sanctimonious judgment of others, and the list goes on? But that's what happens when people walk away from the Lord God and only do what is right in their own eyes. The only solution is personal confession and repentance and trust in the forgiveness that Jesus secured for us on the cross. And, of course, it begins with you and me.

As I was writing this chapter, it struck me that, in

our culture today, we are living in a time so similar to the period of the judges. More and more people are doing what is right in their own eyes, not God's eyes. And our culture is filled with lawlessness, violence, and death as well. Also, as I was preparing this chapter, the US Supreme Court reversed a nearly 50-year-old ruling, *Roe v. Wade*, which stated that abortion was a constitutional right. The 2022 US Supreme Court determined that the *Roe v. Wade* ruling was unconstitutional. There never has been a constitutional right to end another person's life.

It has been pointed out that since *Roe v. Wade* has been the law of the United States, over 63,000,000 babies have been murdered before they could ever be born. Human life in our culture seems to be valued less and less. And it's not just abortion. It's the growing number of murders on our streets and in our communities. It's the intentional lacing of legal and illegal drugs with fentanyl, killing thousands. It's the international trafficking of human beings, especially women. And the list goes on.

But there's more. I'm struck by the response to the Supreme Court's decision. There have been elected officials in one branch of the US government who have publicly stated that they are not going to follow the rightful decision of another branch of government. That's lawlessness. I'm struck by the lawlessness of people protesting and destroying other people's property, not just currently but in the past few years. That's criminal.

I'm weary of hearing about judges and district attorneys who won't prosecute crimes or enforce the law.

And that's my short list.

The lesson to be learned here is that when each person does what is right in his or her own eyes, things will end badly. Just read the book of Judges. Only when we align our lives with the Word and will of our God can we expect his blessing and enjoy peace and prosperity.

God help us!

AHAB AND JEZEBEL

There is a thread that shows up in a few of the crimes we've investigated so far. The thread is this: when one crime is committed, it often leads to other crimes being committed. For example, King David's adultery with Bathsheba led to another crime, David's murder of Uriah the Hittite. But then it also had ramifications within David's family with sons and nephews being murdered and a daughter being raped by her half brother. Or in the last chapter, the death of a single concubine had ramifications that resulted in the deaths of thousands of Israelite soldiers and almost caused an entire Israelite tribe to become extinct. The thread that we've seen repeated is that a single crime can string into other crimes.

That thread shows up again in our next true crime. A single crime of false testimony eventually led to the tragic murders of more than just a few people.

Let's begin with the historical context using King David as the reference point. King David ruled Israel one thousand years before Jesus was born. To be precise, he ruled from 1010 B.C. until 970 B.C.—40 years on the throne. Then his son Solomon ruled as king for the next 41 years. Solomon's son Rehoboam was next in line. He started out as the king of all 12 tribes, but shortly after he ascended to the throne, the northern 10 tribes rebelled and seceded.

The 10 northern tribes became known as Israel, and the 2 southern tribes—Judah and Benjamin—became known as Judah. Recall that Benjamin was the tribe that nearly became extinct. The split into two kingdoms happened in 931 B.C. Now, 60 years later, the seventh king of the northern kingdom of Israel ascended to the throne. His name was King Ahab, and he is at the center of this investigation.

There's no other way to say it. Ahab was a bad dude. In fact, all of the 19 kings who ruled Israel were bad. The Bible tells us they were wicked. King Ahab is described this way: **"Ahab son of Omri did more evil in the eyes of the Lord than any of those before him. He not only considered it trivial to commit the sins of Jeroboam . . ."** (1 Kings 16:30,31). Let's pause here for a second. Jeroboam was the first king of Israel following the split, and Jeroboam's sin was idolatry. He set up two golden calves in Israel, idols made of metal, one in the north at Dan and the other in the south at Bethel. Jeroboam fostered the worship of other gods, not the worship of the Lord. That was the sin of Jeroboam.

Okay, back to Ahab: **"He not only considered it trivial to commit the sins of Jeroboam son of Nebat, but he also married Jezebel daughter of Ethbaal king** of the Sidonians, and began to serve Baal and worship him. He set up an altar for Baal in the temple of Baal that he built in Samaria. Ahab also made an Asherah pole and did more to arouse the anger of the Lord, the God of Israel, than did all the kings of Israel before him" (1 Kings 16:31-33).

King Ahab did evil in the eyes of the Lord because he endorsed and promoted the worship of Baal and Asherah, the fertility god and goddess of the ancient world. His wife, Jezebel, who was a pagan foreigner from the coastal city of Sidon in Phoenicia, had a particular hatred for God's people. She led the charge to kill off all the Lord's prophets in Israel. Ahab may have been a bad dude, but his wife was the wicked witch from the west.

King Ahab ruled Israel during the time of the prophet Elijah. As the mouthpiece for the Lord, Elijah warned King Ahab of the coming judgment if he didn't obey the word of the Lord. Ahab didn't listen. So in his third year reigning as king, the Lord sent Elijah to tell Ahab that there would not be any rain for three and a half years. Then three and a half years later, it was Elijah who challenged Ahab and the 450 prophets of Baal and the 400 prophets of Asherah to a contest on Mt. Carmel located in the northwestern part of Israel. Elijah challenged them to discover who was the true God of Israel, Baal or Yahweh.

There on Mt. Carmel, Elijah set up two altars, one for the prophets of Baal and one for himself. The task was for the prophets of Baal to call out to Baal to send fire to consume the sacrifice. The prophets of Baal were unsuccessful despite their impassioned efforts.

Then it was Elijah's turn. He first had his altar doused with 12 large jars of water. Then he called out to the Lord. The Lord sent fire. It burned up not only the sacrifice but also the wood and the stones and the water in the trench around the altar. The three-and-a-half-year drought ended that day. It was also the day Elijah had the 450 prophets of Baal put to death in an effort to rid the land of the worship of Baal. And it was also the day Elijah had to escape for his life. Queen Jezebel vowed to have Elijah killed because he had put to death all the prophets of Baal.

That's a snapshot of King Ahab and Queen Jezebel. It gives us a sense of the kind of immoral and corrupt people they were. What happened next shouldn't be a surprise to us. What Ahab did, with his wife's help, sealed the Lord's judgment upon him *and* her.

"Some time later there was an incident involving a vineyard belonging to Naboth the Jezreelite. The vineyard was in Jezreel, close to the palace of Ahab king of Samaria" (1 Kings 21:1).

King Ahab came to Naboth, a local vintner, one day with a proposal: **"Let me have your vineyard to use for a vegetable garden, since it is close to my palace. In exchange I will give you a better vineyard or, if you prefer, I will pay you whatever it is worth"** (1 Kings 21:2). Naboth responded to King Ahab's proposal the only way he could. God's Old Testament law did not permit a landowner to sell land that was part of the inheritance handed down from generation to generation. It was to remain in the family. The land was not for sale at any price.

Ahab went home brooding and angry. He went and laid down on his bed. When dinnertime came, Ahab refused to eat. Queen Jezebel noticed that her husband was unhappy, so she asked him what was wrong. Ahab told her about his conversation with Naboth and that he refused to sell his vineyard.

Jezebel told her husband that since he was the king of Israel, he could have anything he wanted:

"Is this how you act as king over Israel? Get up and eat! Cheer up. I'll get you the vineyard of Naboth the Jezreelite."

So she wrote letters in Ahab's name, placed his seal on them, and sent them to the elders and nobles who lived in Naboth's city with him. In those letters she wrote:

"Proclaim a day of fasting and seat Naboth in a prominent place among the people. But seat two scoundrels opposite him and have them bring charges that he has cursed both God and the king. Then take him out and stone him to death." (1 Kings 21:7-10)

Let's examine a little more closely the devious plan of Queen Jezebel. First, she took on the king's identity (today we'd call that identity theft), wrote a letter, and forged her husband's signature using his personal seal. The letter was sent to the elders and nobles of the city. The elders were the oldest and most respected men of the city, and the nobles were members of the ruling class. The letter directed the elders and nobles to declare a day of fasting. This was particularly depraved in that Jezebel was suggesting using a religious ceremony to cover up her murderous plan.

At this ceremony, Jezebel directed the city leaders to find two scoundrels—men with no ethics—to accuse Naboth of cursing God and the king. According to Old Testament law, two eyewitnesses were required to carry out any death sentence. Jezebel's evil plan against Naboth worked just as she planned it. The witnesses falsely accused Naboth, and he was taken outside the city and stoned to death.

"As soon as Jezebel heard that Naboth had been stoned to death, she said to Ahab, 'Get up and take possession of the vineyard of Naboth the Jezreelite that he refused to sell you. He is no longer alive, but dead.' When Ahab heard that Naboth was dead, he got up and went down to take possession of Naboth's vineyard" (1 Kings 21:15,16). Did you catch that? Even after Naboth was dead, the biblical text still refers to the vineyard as Naboth's.

Because of Ahab's and Jezebel's heinous crimes

against Naboth, God condemned them both. The Lord sent the prophet Elijah to speak to Ahab: **"Go down to meet Ahab king of Israel, who rules in Samaria. He is now in Naboth's vineyard, where he has gone to take possession of it"** (1 Kings 21:18). Imagine that! Elijah confronted Ahab in the vineyard that he had stolen from Naboth after murdering him.

> "Say to him, 'This is what the Lord says: Have you not murdered a man and seized his property?' Then say to him, 'This is what the Lord says: In the place where dogs licked up Naboth's blood, dogs will lick up your blood—yes, yours!'"
>
> Ahab said to Elijah, "So you have found me, my enemy!"
>
> "I have found you," he answered, "because you have sold yourself to do evil in the eyes of the Lord. He says, 'I am going to bring disaster on you. I will wipe out your descendants and cut off from Ahab every last male in Israel—slave or free. I will make your house like that of Jeroboam son of Nebat and that of Baasha son of Ahijah, because you have aroused my anger and have caused Israel to sin.'
>
> "And also concerning Jezebel the Lord says:

'Dogs will devour Jezebel by the wall of Jezreel.'

"Dogs will eat those belonging to Ahab who die in the city, and the birds will feed on those who die in the country." (1 Kings 21:19-24)

Ahab considered Elijah his enemy, and Ahab was also an enemy of the Lord God because he had sold himself to evil. The disaster that the Lord promised to come upon Ahab and Jezebel revealed that preserving life and the property rights of others are important to the Lord. According to the book of Proverbs, **"there are six things the Lord hates, seven that are detestable to him: haughty eyes** (in other words pride)**, a lying tongue, hands that shed innocent blood, a heart that devises wicked schemes, feet that are quick to rush into evil, a false witness who pours out lies and a person who stirs up conflict in the community"** (6:16-19).

By my count, Ahab and Jezebel were clearly guilty of five of the seven things that the Lord hates.

Elijah's pronouncement of judgment on Ahab and Jezebel shook Ahab to the core. He was remorseful. He tore his clothes, a sign of mourning, grief, or loss. He put on sackcloth, a sign of submission and humility. And Ahab also fasted, a way to humble oneself before the Lord. The Lord took notice of this change. As a result, the Lord's judgment would not come to Ahab's descendants during his lifetime but would be delayed until after his death. Despite Ahab being a wicked man, the Lord still showed him mercy. Ahab would not have to witness the death of his sons.

For the next three years, the nation of Israel was not at war with their perennial enemy, the nation of Aram. Aram was located to the northeast of Israel, also known as Syria, with Damascus as its capital. Previously, Ahab and his army had defeated the Syrian army, led by King Ben-Hadad. In that battle, the Lord had instructed Ahab to end the life of Ben-Hadad to bring lasting peace to Israel. Ahab disobeyed and instead made a treaty with the defeated king. Bad move.

One day the king of the southern tribe of Judah, King Jehoshaphat, was invited to meet with Ahab in Samaria. Ahab had a lavish banquet prepared for Jehoshaphat and his entourage. We learn from 2 Chronicles chapter 18 that there was a marriage alliance between Ahab and Jehoshaphat. Jehoshaphat, who was a god-fearing king, unfortunately helped arrange a marriage between his son Jehoram and Athaliah, the daughter of Ahab and Jezebel, a wicked woman who took after her mother.

Ahab pointed out to Jehoshaphat that the city of Ramoth Gilead, on the east side of the Jordan River, had previously been captured by the Syrian army. Ahab wanted it back and asked Jehoshaphat and the army of Judah to go to war to reclaim it. Having lost Ramoth Gilead, a city originally given as part of the Promised Land, was an embarrassment that both kings wanted to correct. But before agreeing to the alliance, Jehoshaphat wanted to inquire of the Lord, Yahweh.

Ahab summoned four hundred prophets to give advice as to whether to go to war or not. They said yes, **"for the Lord will give it into the king's hand"** (1 Kings 22:6). What Ahab's prophets didn't say is significant. When they said, "The Lord will give it into the king's hand," the word they used for *Lord* was not *Yahweh*. These four hundred prophets were not prophets of the Lord God. That led Jehoshaphat to ask, **"Is there no longer a prophet of the Lord** (Yahweh) **here whom we can inquire of?"** (1 Kings 22:7). There was a prophet of Yahweh, named Micaiah, who was in prison for telling Ahab past unfavorable messages from the Lord God.

Micaiah was summoned and did not have a favorable report for Ahab. In fact, Micaiah said that Ahab would be killed in this battle and his army routed.

Despite Micaiah's words from the Lord, Ahab and Jehoshaphat went to battle for Ramoth Gilead. Ahab disguised himself as a common soldier, not wearing his royal robes so as not to stick out for Aram's army to target him. The king of Aram had told his charioteers, "Don't fight anyone else. Just get King Ahab." The charioteers didn't kill Ahab though. Ahab's death is described this way, which demonstrates the hand of the Lord: **"Someone drew his bow at random and hit the king of Israel between the sections of his armor"** (1 Kings 22:34). Coincidence? Lucky shot? Not at all. The Lord God determined that this was the day Ahab's time of grace on this earth would end.

King Ahab told his chariot driver to get him out of

there. He was wounded. That day Ahab died, was taken back to Samaria, and buried. Because there was a lot of blood in his chariot, some soldiers took it to a pool in Samaria where prostitutes bathed, and the soldiers washed it out. Wild dogs came and licked up the blood, just as the word of the Lord had declared. The Lord was true to his word.

Wicked Queen Jezebel lived for approximately ten more years. Jezebel's son Ahaziah became king and ruled for just two years. He had an injury from a fall and never recovered from it because he consulted with Baal and not Yahweh. Because Ahaziah had no son, his brother Joram ascended to the throne. Joram was as wicked as his father and brother, no doubt also under the influence of Mama Jezebel.

During this time, the prophet Elijah's successor, Elisha, was tasked by the Lord God to anoint a military commander by the name of Jehu to become king of Israel. This prompted a civil war in Israel between Joram and Jehu. Jehu killed Joram—guess where?—at the site of Naboth's vineyard. From there Jehu headed to Jezebel's palace in Jezreel. When Jezebel heard Jehu was coming, we're told she adorned herself for the occasion, putting on makeup, styling her hair, and looking out the window to see Jehu coming.

Looking down from her window, Jezebel taunted him, so Jehu ordered her eunuchs, castrated male servants, to throw her out the window. They did, and she was trampled by the soldiers' horses. Later, when Jehu commanded that she be properly buried as a king's daughter, it was discovered that dogs had eaten most of her body. All that was left was her skull, hands, and feet. From Jezreel, Jehu headed to the city of Samaria, where the rest of King Ahab's family were put to death. The Lord God was true to his word. Naboth's death was finally avenged.

The lesson to be learned here is summed up in the First Commandment: "You shall have no other gods." When we serve the Lord God and follow his will for our lives, we will experience his amazing grace and blessing. If we don't, however, we risk the same fate as Ahab and Jezebel. The encouragement we take away from this story is to love the Lord our God and serve him only.

THE HERODS

This chapter is somewhat unique. We're going to investigate two separate crimes committed 30 years apart. One was a mass murder. The other was the murder of a single individual. But these two crimes, separated by three decades, have some things in common. The first crime was committed by a man named Herod. The second crime was committed by a man named Herod. But they weren't the same Herod. They were father and son.

The father was Herod I, also known as Herod the Great. The son was Herod Antipas. The murders they committed reveal some similarities as to the thinking and motivation of both Herods. Both kings had a lust for power. It should come as no surprise that the desire for power is a very powerful human emotion and can lead people to take drastic action, either to acquire power in the first place or to keep their hold on it.

These two Herods show up on the pages of the Bible. But before we get to their stories, it would be helpful to learn more about them. And here's why. Who they were and how they came to their thrones reveals the source of their power, how fragile that power was, and why they took such drastic steps to hold on to it. Much of what we know about the Herods is from the historian Josephus and, to a lesser degree, the historian Appian. If you aren't a history nerd, hang in there with me. I think you'll appreciate the historical context for what the Bible tells us about these two Herods.

Here's a trivia question for you. What was the ethnic and nationality background of Herod the Great and his successors? It would be perfectly reasonable to assume that because Herod was a king ruling on behalf of the Roman Empire that he was a Roman. Good guess, but no cigar.

Herod's parents were actually from the country of Edom, which was a border nation located to the southeast of Judea. Ethnically, Herod's parents were Arabs or Nabataeans as some scholars suggest. Nabataeans were a Bedouin tribe that roamed the Arabian Peninsula. But get this, somewhere in Herod's family history, his ancestors converted to Judaism. So Herod was raised a Jew and considered himself a Jew. That makes a lot of sense from a Roman Empire perspective. Who better to be king over the Jews than someone who himself was a Jew?

Herod the Great was born around 72 B.C. His father was a high-ranking government official who had a good relationship with Julius Caesar, the Roman general who led the Roman armies in the Gallic Wars and who defeated his archrival, Pompey, in a civil war. As a result, Julius Caesar became dictator in 49 B.C. and ruled five years until he was assassinated in 44 B.C. Kings and dictators faced the chronic threat of an assassination attempt by a rival who was seeking his own power.

Julius Caesar, before his death, had entrusted Herod's father with overseeing all the public affairs in Judea. A couple of years later, Herod himself was appointed governor of the province of Galilee. Herod would have been about 25 years old at the time. Herod's ascent to a governorship was an example of not what you know but who you know.

Then in 41 B.C., the Roman ruler Mark Antony—yes, the Mark Antony of Antony and Cleopatra fame—appointed Herod as a tetrarch (ruler over a province) to support Rome's appointed ruler of Judea. The ruler's name was Hyrcanus II. He ruled from Jerusalem. When Hyrcanus was overthrown by his own nephew, Antigonus, Herod went to Rome to advocate that the Roman leaders restore Hyrcanus to power. They didn't. But then, in a surprising move, the Roman Senate in 37 B.C. appointed Herod to be the king of the Jews, not a religious title but a political one.

Herod left Rome and returned to Judea; after a three-year war, he defeated Antigonus and secured for himself kingship over Jerusalem and all Judea. He would rule Judea as a subordinate, client state of the Roman Empire until his death.

As I mentioned before, Herod I was also known as Herod the Great. What made him great? One of the key contributing factors to his title were his massive building projects that he planned and completed all across Judea. A couple of them were for the benefit of the Jewish people; others were for his own personal prestige and safety.

Around 19 B.C., he began an expansion project on the Temple Mount in Jerusalem. Not only did he rebuild and enlarge the Jewish temple; he expanded the earthen platform on which the temple stood so that the platform was twice the size of the original. If you go to Jerusalem and visit the Western Wall, you'll witness evidence of Herod's building project. The Western Wall was part of the perimeter wall of the expanded platform that Herod had constructed. This was Herod's most ambitious building project.

Another of Herod's building projects was at the Cave of the Patriarchs in Hebron. The patriarch Abraham had originally purchased the land that had this cave. Abraham wanted to bury his wife, Sarah, there. When Abraham died, Isaac and Ishmael buried him there as well. Isaac; Isaac's wife, Rebekah; Esau; and Jacob were all buried there too. So it was named the Cave of the Patriarchs. For the Jewish people, this was a sacred site. The building project that Herod commissioned was to build a large rectangular enclosure over the cave to commemorate the site for the Jewish people. Fun fact—the stone walls of this structure were six feet thick.

The coastal city of Caesarea was home to four different building projects commissioned by Herod. First, there was Herod's Harbor. He built a 40-acre harbor that would accommodate three hundred ships. In Caesarea, he also constructed an outdoor theater with a seating capacity of 3,500. And, of course, King Herod needed a royal palace overlooking the Mediterranean Sea. It was called the Promontory Palace because it was built on a promontory jutting out into the sea. What was unique in the palace was a very large swimming pool filled with fresh water. But to get the fresh water, Herod also built an aqueduct from springs located at the base of Mt. Carmel about ten miles away. In order to have gravity move the water, the aqueduct was built on arches and was constructed with a precise gradient so the water would flow at just the right rate.

Then there were the five fortresses that Herod built, fortresses for himself and his family in the event of an insurrection. The most well-known of these fortresses is Masada. Today Masada is the most popular tourist site in Israel.

All these building projects contributed to Herod being called Herod the Great. But he did more than that. Herod also provided for the people living in Judea during difficult times, especially during famines. Herod, for the most part, was a king who cared for the people of Judea.

But he did things that upset the Jewish people, especially the religious leaders. All his building projects, as great as they were, required capital to fund them. Much of it came in the form of taxes. Herod's taxes were despised, as were the tax collectors who collected them.

When the temple was being rebuilt, Herod ignored the demands of the Jewish religious leaders regarding the construction. He also replaced the local religious leaders with priests from Babylon and Egypt to win the favor of Jews living in these foreign countries. Despite the good that Herod did, there was a strong national sentiment to overthrow Rome's control. The Jewish people were looking for a savior from Roman rule.

What's even worse is that Herod had a really dark side. Herod was chronically paranoid. He was always concerned that someone was coming to take him out, to assassinate him. Maybe that's why he thought he needed five fortresses. Some of his concern was justified. It was not uncommon for kings to be assassinated by a rival to the throne. But Herod's concern for his own safety went to the extreme.

During his reign, he had several high-ranking officials put to death because he sensed they were a threat to his throne. He had several of his own family members executed, including one of his ten wives along with her son and her mother, who was actually seeking to unseat him. He had a brother-in-law put to death and even two of his own sons, Alexander and Aristobulus. To protect himself, Herod had a personal bodyguard. Would you believe his bodyguard consisted of two thousand soldiers? Herod had secret police to monitor and investigate what the people were saying about him. Herod the Great or Herod the Paranoid?

That's a little bit about Herod the Great—the good, the bad, and now let's get to the ugly:

After Jesus was born in Bethlehem in Judea, during the time of King Herod, Magi from the east came to Jerusalem and asked, "Where is the one who has been born king of the Jews? We saw his star when it rose and have come to worship him."

When King Herod heard this he was disturbed, and all Jerusalem with him. When he had called together all the people's chief priests and teachers of the law, he asked them where the Messiah was to be born. "In Bethlehem in Judea," they replied. (Matthew 2:1-5)

Nearly 40 years earlier, the Roman Senate declared Herod to be the king of the Jews. And now, some dudes from out East came looking for one who had been *born* king of the Jews? So it isn't a surprise that Herod was disturbed. His paranoia kicked into high gear. **"Then Herod called the Magi secretly and found out from them the exact time the star had appeared. He sent them to Bethlehem and said, 'Go and search carefully for the child. As soon as you find him, report to me, so that I too may go and worship him'"** (Matthew 2:7,8).

The Magi left and headed to Bethlehem, where they found Mary and Joseph and the baby Jesus. They worshiped him and presented their gifts of gold, frankincense, and myrrh. Then in a dream, the Magi were warned not to return to Herod and to head home a different way. In another dream, an angel of the Lord appeared to Joseph and told him to flee to Egypt because Herod was going to search for Jesus and kill him.

"When Herod realized that he had been outwitted by the Magi, he was furious, and he gave orders to kill all the boys in Bethlehem and its vicinity who were two years old and under, in accordance with the time he had learned from the Magi" (Matthew 2:16). Herod's paranoia drove him to become a baby killer. This tragic event has been called "the slaughter of the innocence." Herod the Great? Herod the Paranoid? How about Herod the Murderer? Fear and paranoia are strong human emotions. They can lead us to do drastic things, irrational things, destructive things. We would do well to recognize our own fears and paranoia and control them so that they don't control us.

When Herod the Great died, the Romans divided his kingdom among three of his sons and his sister: Archelaus became ethnarch of Judea, Samaria, and Idumea; Herod Antipas became ruler of Galilee and Perea; Philip became ruler of territories north and east of the Jordan, which today is called the Golan Heights; and Salome was given what's called a toparchy—a small district that had several cities. This succession plan was devised by Herod the Great but had to be ratified by Caesar Augustus, also known as Octavian, who ruled as the first Roman Emperor from 27 B.C. to A.D. 14. Caesar Augustus for the most part approved Herod's succession plan.

Now meet Herod Antipas.

Herod Antipas was born about 20 years before Jesus was born. Herod Antipas is referred to both in history books and the Bible as Herod the Tetrarch. He never officially had the title of king. The two regions that Herod Antipas ruled were Galilee in the north and Perea, which was on the eastern side of the Jordan River. The two regions were separated by a piece of real estate known as the Decapolis. The Decapolis was a region comprised of ten cities, nine of which were on the east side of the Jordan with one city on the west. The area around the city on the west side was what separated Galilee from Perea.

After Herod the Great died, which created a short-term leadership vacuum, there were multiple revolts. One took place at the palace of Sepphoris in Galilee. Herod Antipas was in Rome when this occurred. The historian Josephus wrote that a Jewish zealot by the name of Judas son of Hezekiah attacked Sepphoris, plundered the city, taking money and weapons that were used to terrorize the region. The Roman governor in Syria responded to this revolt by burning the city and selling its inhabitants into slavery.

When Herod Antipas assumed his reign as tetrarch, he followed in his father's footsteps. He rebuilt and fortified the city of Sepphoris. He also fortified the city of Betharamphtha in Perea. But Herod Antipas' greatest construction project was building his capital city of Tiberias on the western shores of the Sea of Galilee. One of the features of this city was the nearby access to 17 mineral hot springs. He also built a stadium, a palace, and a sanctuary for Jewish prayer. Tiberias became the largest city and one of the most important cities in Galilee. It's mentioned in John chapter 6 as the location from which boats sailed to the eastern shore of the Sea of Galilee after Jesus' miraculous feeding of the five thousand.

In Matthew chapter 14, we read about Herod Antipas' previous interaction with John the Baptist. It's a section that recaps what happened to John the Baptist at the hands of Herod Antipas. **"At that time Herod the tetrarch heard the reports about Jesus, and he said to his attendants, 'This is John the Baptist; he has risen from the dead! That is why miraculous powers are at work in him'"** (verses 1,2).

A few things to point out. First, John the Baptist was already dead. Second, Herod Antipas learned about Jesus and his miraculous powers and acknowledged Jesus' ability to perform miracles. And third, Herod must have had a guilty conscience because he assumed that Jesus was really John the Baptist back from the dead in order to haunt him.

Here's what happened between John the Baptist and Herod Antipas. **"Now Herod had arrested John and bound him and put him in prison because of**

Herodias, his brother Philip's wife" (Matthew 14:3). Let's just pause here for a moment. The relationship between Herod Antipas and Herodias is a bit complicated, but I'll do my best to uncomplicate it.

Early in his reign, Herod Antipas was married to the daughter of Aretas, the king of Nabataea. Recall that the Nabataeans were a nomad tribe living in the desert of Arabia. The daughter's name was Phasaelis. However, on a trip to Rome, Herod Antipas stayed with his half brother Philip (same father, different mothers; remember Philip was the ruler of what today is the Golan Heights). While in Rome, Herod Antipas fell in love with Philip's wife, Herodias. Keep in mind that Philip and Herodias had a daughter named Salome. More on her in a bit. Now Herodias was the granddaughter of Herod the Great, so Philip wasn't only her husband; he was also her uncle—Uncle Phil. That also meant that Herod Antipas was Herodias' half uncle. What a tangled web!

Herod Antipas and Herodias ran off together and headed back to Galilee. They agreed to get married as soon as Herod Antipas divorced his wife, Phasaelis. Phasaelis finagled a way to return to her father, King Aretas. Once she was under the safety of her father, King Aretas waged war against Herod Antipas, a war that Herod Antipas would eventually lose to be followed by a charge of treason by one of his own nephews.

Back to Matthew's account: **"Now Herod had arrested John and bound him and put him in prison because of Herodias, his brother Philip's wife, for**

John had been saying to him: 'It is not lawful for you to have her.' Herod wanted to kill John, but he was afraid of the people, because they considered John a prophet" (14:3-5). John the Baptist publicly criticized Herod Antipas for taking his brother's wife to be his own. To shut John up, Herod Antipas had John thrown into prison. Historians indicate that this was at one of the palaces/fortresses that Herod the Great had built. It was the Machaerus fortress on the eastern bank of the Dead Sea.

> **On Herod's birthday the daughter of Herodias** (this would have been Salome) **danced for the guests and pleased Herod so much that he promised with an oath to give her whatever she asked. Prompted by her mother, she said, "Give me here on a platter the head of John the Baptist." The king was distressed, but because of his oaths and his dinner guests, he ordered that her request be granted and had John beheaded in the prison. His head was brought in on a platter and given to the girl, who carried it to her mother. John's disciples came and took his body and buried it. Then they went and told Jesus.** (Matthew 14:6-12)

There is so much wrong with what Herod Antipas, Herodias, and Salome did. Herod Antipas' recklessness, foolishness, and unwillingness to do what was right just to save face with his guests cost John the Baptist his life. Like his father, Herod Antipas was a murderer.

But that's not the end of Herod Antipas' story. During Jesus' final ministry in Galilee, a group of Pharisees warned Jesus that Herod was plotting his death. Do you recall Jesus' response? **"He replied, 'Go tell that fox, "I will keep on driving out demons and healing people today and tomorrow, and on the third day I will reach my goal." In any case, I must press on today and tomorrow and the next day—for surely no prophet can die outside Jerusalem!'"** (Luke 13:32,33).

Jesus was headed to Jerusalem, where he was betrayed, arrested, and brought before Pontius Pilate for trial. Jesus was brought before Pilate because he was the governor of Roman Judea, which included Jerusalem where Jesus was arrested. Because Jesus had been so active in Galilee and Herod Antipas was in Jerusalem that week, Pilate sent him to Herod Antipas. Herod wanted to see Jesus perform a miracle, but Jesus did not oblige him. So Herod sent Jesus back to Pilate's court having found nothing deserving of death. That's the last time we hear of Herod Antipas in the New Testament.

Mark Twain's character Huck Finn said, "All kings is mostly rapscallions." A rapscallion is a person who causes trouble. That was certainly the case of the two Herods.

For each of us, we need to be aware that having a position of authority has the potential for causing trouble. For example, parents who are overly controlling of their children can result in those children becoming bitter and rebellious. Or a boss who has a heavy hand and is overly demanding of his or her employees can result in a lack of motivation and poor performance. Or a politician who will do anything to stay in power can cause distrust among the people he or she is elected to serve. Having power or a position of authority has the potential for trouble.

Only when we submit our lives to the King of kings and trust in Jesus for forgiveness can any of us escape being a rapscallion.

PAUL

So far we've investigated nine crimes committed by people in the Bible. We've noted along the way that the Lord God responded to these crimes in different ways—sometimes with judgment, sometimes with grace and mercy. For those who despised the Lord God, the response was typically judgment. For those who believed in the Lord God, the response was typically grace and mercy. That's something we need to keep in mind. The Lord God shows grace and mercy to those who acknowledge him as the Lord of heaven and earth.

In this chapter, we will investigate a crime committed by a man who was considered public enemy #1 by Jesus' followers. He was a deeply religious man, an educated man, a man who loved the Old Testament law, and a man who hated Jesus. At his birth, his parents gave him the name Saul. We first want to look at Saul's background and education because they give us insight into who he was and what motivated him to commit the crimes he did.

We learn about Saul from two places in the Bible. One source is the book of Acts, written by Dr. Luke, who chronicled the life of the early church, especially the missionary journeys of the apostles. The other source is from the letters written by the apostle Paul who, earlier in his life, had been the murderer Saul. Saul the murderer and Paul the missionary were one in the same, separated by a miraculous conversion.

According to historians, Saul was likely born between 5 B.C. and A.D. 5, making him a Jewish contemporary of Jesus. Saul was born in the city of Tarsus, which is located about 12 miles inland from the Mediterranean Sea in the southeast corner of what today is the country of Turkey. During the Roman Empire, Tarsus was the capital city of the Roman province of Cilicia, a significant city in terms of trade, culture, education, and influence. Tarsus had been an influential city in Asia Minor ever since the days of the Greek ruler Alexander the Great. And keep in mind that Alexander the Great died in 323 B.C.

Ten years before Alexander died, he marched through Tarsus with his army as he was conquering the known world. He stopped in Tarsus and took a dip, or bath, in the temperature-challenged Cydnus River. When he entered the cold river, his limbs and joints became stiff. His servants had to carry him out of the river. He was ill for many days and almost died. Imagine if he had; how world history would have changed! For more than three hundred years, Tarsus was a Greek city, aka a Hellenized city, of influence in terms of east/west trade, advanced education, and contemporary Greek culture.

Tarsus was home to many philosophers, poets, and literary scholars. The schools of Tarsus had a great reputation. They rivaled the schools of Athens, Greece, and Alexandria, Egypt. There was a library in Tarsus that had 200,000 books, including not only literary works but scientific works as well! Tarsus was no average city. The apostle Paul even mentioned this fact recorded in the book of Acts.

At the conclusion of his third missionary journey, Paul traveled back to Jerusalem. There he was confronted by Jews from Asia Minor, present-day Turkey, who stirred up the Jerusalem crowds against him. They grabbed him in the temple and dragged him outside in order to kill him. Word reached the Roman troops stationed nearby that there was a riot in the streets. The troops came and essentially rescued Paul from imminent death and took him away to their garrison.

Before entering the garrison, Paul asked the commander if he could address the crowd. The commander initially mistook Paul for an Egyptian fugitive who had previously led a revolt and then led four thousand terrorists out into the desert. Paul replied in Greek, "No, no, that's not me."

Then he described himself: **"I am a Jew, from Tarsus in Cilicia, a citizen of no ordinary city. Please let me speak to the people"** (Acts 21:39). For Paul to say that he was a citizen of no ordinary city was another way of saying, "I'm a citizen of a very important city." By the way, the commander allowed Paul to speak to the Jewish crowds. When he did, he didn't speak in Greek but in Aramaic. Aramaic was the language spoken by the Jews in Jesus' day. In Old Testament times, the Israelites spoke Hebrew. Hebrew and Aramaic are similar languages, sometimes called sister languages. And of all the Semitic languages in the ancient world, only two are still spoken today—Hebrew and Aramaic.

Although Tarsus was a Greek city for three centuries that reflected Greek culture, when the Romans became the world's only superpower, it was the Roman general Pompey who gained control of Tarsus and made it subject to Rome in the year 67 B.C. It was under Pompey that Tarsus became the capital city of the province of Cilicia. Yes, indeed, a very important city.

In Tarsus, Saul grew up in a devout Jewish family. In his letter to the Christians living in the Greek city of Philippi, we learn more about his roots. The situation in Philippi was that there was a group of people known as the Judaizers who were becoming an increasing threat to the Christians living there. The Judaizers were either Jewish or Gentile converts to Christianity. They claimed to believe in Jesus as their Lord and Savior but also insisted that the Old Testament laws of Moses be followed to the letter, especially the requirement for circumcision.

Judaizers were especially proud of their Jewishness because they prided themselves in living according to Jewish laws and customs. The apostle Paul addressed this idea of Jewishness by pointing out that he personally had as much Jewishness as anyone. This is what he wrote: **"If someone else thinks they have reasons to put confidence in the flesh, I have more: circumcised on the eighth day, of the people of Israel, of the tribe of Benjamin, a Hebrew of Hebrews; in regard to the law, a Pharisee; as for zeal, persecuting the church; as for righteousness based on the law, faultless"** (Philippians 3:4-6).

All these descriptive phrases are worth exploring a bit more because they give added insight into why Saul persecuted and murdered Christians.

"Circumcised on the eighth day, of the people of Israel": Paul was born a Jew and was circumcised on the eighth day after birth as prescribed by Old Testament law. This entitled him to all the benefits and privileges given to God's Old Testament chosen people.

"Of the tribe of Benjamin, a Hebrew of Hebrews": Not only was Paul of the people of Israel; he was also from the tribe of Benjamin. The tribe of Benjamin was significant among the Jews for several reasons. When the Assyrians invaded and took the northern 10 tribes into captivity, the tribe of Benjamin joined the tribe of Judah and was spared from the Assyrian assault. And then, after the Babylonian captivity, the only 2 tribes to remain out of the original 12 were Benjamin and Judah, which became known as the land of Judea.

Here's a trivia question for you. Is the city of Jerusalem located in the tribe of Benjamin or in the tribe of Judah? In the book of Joshua, there is one reference to Jerusalem being in the tribal boundaries of Benjamin and another reference to it being in the tribe of Judah. So the answer is *yes*.

Jerusalem was located on the border of the tribes of Benjamin and Judah. The tribe of Benjamin could legitimately claim the capital city of Jerusalem as being in their tribe. But Judah could make that claim as well. In fact, there's a Jewish tradition which claims that the altars and sanctuary of the temple in Jerusalem were located in the tribe of Benjamin, whereas the courts of the temple were located in the tribe of Judah. Just a tradition.

Another feather in the cap of the tribe of Benjamin was that Benjamin's mother was Rachel, the patriarch Jacob's favorite wife who also gave birth to Joseph, who became the number-two ruler in Egypt. And finally, Israel's first king came from the tribe of Benjamin, King Saul, after whom the first-century Saul was likely named.

When Paul mentioned being a Hebrew of Hebrews, it suggested that he and his family didn't just speak Greek and/or Aramaic like most other people. When it came especially to their religious expressions and worship, they actually spoke Hebrew.

"*In regard to the law, a Pharisee*": The Pharisees were the teachers of Israel, and there were two aspects of Jewish life that the Pharisees were especially committed to—the Old Testament law and the temple. We see that emphasis in Jesus' interaction with the Pharisees during his ministry. The Pharisees repeatedly challenged Jesus about his and his disciples not keeping the Old Testament law, especially the laws governing the Sabbath. Saul laid claim to the fact that not only was he a Pharisee, but he cherished and lived out the Old Testament law as a Pharisee.

"As for zeal, persecuting the church": The word that Paul used for "zeal" referred to harassment that included violence. Saul was willing to use violence to enforce the Law of Moses. This led Saul to persecute the Christ followers because he thought they were blasphemers, that they were mockers of the Lord God of the Old Testament.

"As for righteousness based on the law, faultless": Paul claimed that he followed the Old Testament laws completely. That meant he offered sacrifices as the Old Testament prescribed and studied the books of Moses, the Torah. He lived according to all the ceremonial laws. When he was Saul, he was a poster child for what it meant to be a Jew and a Pharisee.

After Paul rattled off his qualifications for his Jewishness, he completely discounted his past qualifications. This is what he said: **"But whatever were gains to me I now consider loss for the sake of Christ"** (Philippians 3:7). All his Jewishness of the past meant nothing now that he followed Jesus.

While Saul was quite young, his family sent him to Jerusalem to receive his education at the school of Gamaliel. Gamaliel was a Pharisee and a scholar with expertise in the Old Testament law. Gamaliel was also a member of the Sanhedrin, the Jewish ruling council. He was highly respected by the Jewish people and the other religious leaders. When Paul was arrested in Jerusalem, which I referenced earlier, and addressed the people, he mentioned Gamaliel: **"I am a Jew, born in Tarsus of Cilicia, but brought up in this city. I studied under Gamaliel and was thoroughly trained in the law of our ancestors. I was just as zealous for God as any of you are today"** (Acts 22:3).

We first learn about Gamaliel in Acts chapter 5. The story of Gamaliel here isn't pertinent to Saul's crimes, but it's a story worth mentioning. Jesus' apostles had been teaching in Jerusalem and healing people. This caused great jealousy among the Pharisees and other religious leaders. So they threw the apostles in jail. That night an angel busted them out of jail, and the next day they were back in the temple teaching about Jesus. So the religious leaders had them arrested again and brought before the Sanhedrin, the Jewish ruling council. The sentiment among the group was to kill the apostles. But then Gamaliel spoke up:

> **But a Pharisee named Gamaliel, a teacher of the law, who was honored by all the people, stood up in the Sanhedrin and ordered that the men be put outside for a little while. Then he addressed the Sanhedrin: "Men of Israel, consider carefully what you intend to do to these men. Some time ago Theudas appeared,**

claiming to be somebody, and about four hundred men rallied to him. He was killed, all his followers were dispersed, and it all came to nothing. After him, Judas the Galilean appeared in the days of the census and led a band of people in revolt. He too was killed, and all his followers were scattered. Therefore, in the present case I advise you: Leave these men alone! Let them go! For if their purpose or activity is of human origin, it will fail. But if it is from God, you will not be able to stop these men; you will only find yourselves fighting against God." (Acts 5:34-39)

What wise advice Gamaliel offered! As the Jewish religious leaders would discover in the years and decades to come, what Jesus' disciples were teaching and doing was indeed God's doing.

It was this Gamaliel whom Saul studied under and who was influenced by his emphasis on the Old Testament law. Saul became zealous to keep and protect the law. I hope this background about Saul, his family, and his education provides some insight into Saul's motives and actions in persecuting the followers of Jesus.

We first meet Saul in Acts chapter 6 in connection with one of Jesus' followers, a man by the name of Stephen. Stephen is described as **"a man full of God's grace and power, performed great wonders and signs among the people. Opposition arose, however, from** members of the Synagogue of the Freedmen (as it was called)—Jews of Cyrene and Alexandria as well as the provinces of Cilicia and Asia—who began to argue with Stephen. But they could not stand up against the wisdom the Spirit gave him as he spoke"** (verses 8-10).

Did you catch that? Jews from Egypt and the Roman provinces of Cilicia and Asia. And guess who called the province of Cilicia his home? Saul. I've always wondered whether Saul was one of the Jews who argued with Stephen or whether he was just a quiet bystander. The Bible doesn't tell us, so we won't make any assumptions.

When these Jews couldn't stand up to Stephen's Spirit-filled words, they accused him of blasphemy against Moses and against God. They seized Stephen and brought him before the Sanhedrin accusing him of **"speaking against this holy place** (the temple) **and against the law. For we have heard him say that this Jesus of Nazareth will destroy this place and change the customs Moses handed down to us"** (Acts 6:13,14).

What followed was a lengthy address by Stephen in which he recounted Old Testament history—Abraham, Isaac, Jacob, and Moses—and how the Old Testament Israelites repeatedly rejected the Lord God's prophets and leaders. Stephen then called out the religious leaders of his day for rejecting and murdering the very Son of God. Because of what he said and what he saw when he looked to the heavens, the crowd dragged him out of the city and stoned him to death.

Here in Acts we learn that Saul was at the stoning of

Stephen, giving his approval. To give one's approval to a killing meant that Saul had a position of leadership and authority. Now one might be inclined to say, "Well, that's not so bad. At least Saul didn't pick up stones to hurl at Stephen." Maybe so, but in his letter to the Christians living in Galatia, Saul makes a full confession of his crimes:

> I want you to know, brothers and sisters, that the gospel I preached is not of human origin. I did not receive it from any man, nor was I taught it; rather, I received it by revelation from Jesus Christ.
>
> For you have heard of my previous way of life in Judaism, how intensely I persecuted the church of God and tried to destroy it. I was advancing in Judaism beyond many of my own age among my people and was extremely zealous for the traditions of my fathers. (Galatians 1:11-14)

Paul confessed that when he was Saul, he tried to annihilate the church of God by destroying the people of Christ. On the day that Stephen was stoned to death, a great persecution broke out against the church in Jerusalem. Acts chapter 8 tells us that **"Saul began to destroy the church. Going from house to house, he dragged off men and women and put them in prison"** (verse 3).

On one occasion, Saul left Jerusalem and headed to Damascus in Syria. He went with the intention of arresting the Christians there and bringing them back to Jerusalem to be imprisoned.

On that road to Damascus, the Lord Jesus appeared to him:

"Saul, Saul, why do you persecute me?"

"Who are you, Lord?" Saul asked.

"I am Jesus, whom you are persecuting," he replied. "Now get up and go into the city, and you will be told what you must do." (Acts 9:4-6)

Saul had to be led by others into the city because he was blind.

After three days, the Lord Jesus sent a disciple named Ananias to restore Saul's eyesight so he could see again and be filled with the Holy Spirit. In Paul's letter to the Galatians, he described his experience this way: **"But when God, who set me apart from my mother's womb and called me by his grace, was pleased to reveal his Son in me so that I might preach him among the Gentiles, my immediate response was not to consult any human being"** (Galatians 1:15,16). The murderer Saul was called by God's grace to proclaim the name of Jesus to the Gentile world.

The life of Saul turned Paul is one of the most

powerful stories of God's grace in the New Testament. Just think of it. The Lord Jesus appeared one day to Saul, Christian enemy #1, who was seeking to destroy the church of God. Through an act of grace, this Christ-hating Pharisee became the New Testament's greatest missionary of Christ. It's only God's grace that could have converted Saul to Paul.

God's grace is never deserved. Saul didn't deserve it, and we don't deserve it either. But because of Jesus, God gives us his grace freely and fully. Take a moment today to give thanks that God demonstrates his grace to people like Saul and people like you and me.

CONCLUSION

Obviously, these ten criminal acts aren't the only ones in the Bible. There are scores more. They are representative, however, of the crimes recorded in the Bible.

Individuals and groups of people who did not fear the true God committed some of these crimes. In general, God responded to their crimes with judgement. Think of people like Cain, Ahab and Jezebel, and the two Herods. This is an important lesson we want to learn.

Individuals or groups of people who feared and loved the Lord God of heaven and earth committed some of these crimes too. God often responded to their crimes with grace and mercy. Think of Moses, David, and Saul who became Paul. This is another lesson we want to learn.

A third lesson to be learned is the disastrous impact criminal activity can have on oneself, one's family, and even one's nation. Think of David and his family. Think of the Levite and his concubine and the genocide of the tribe of Benjamin.

Another lesson that we learn from these crime stories is the integrity and courage of people who follow the Lord God and set a great example. Think of Uriah, Ehud, Deborah, Jael, and Naboth. They are people worth imitating.

The final lesson we learn from these ten stories is that you and I personally have the capacity to repeat any of these criminal activities. Jesus reminded us of where all criminal activity originates: **"He [Jesus] went on: 'What comes out of a person is what defiles them. For it is from within, out of a person's heart, that evil thoughts come—sexual immorality, theft, murder, adultery, greed, malice, deceit, lewdness, envy, slander, arrogance and folly. All these evils come from inside and defile a person'"** (Mark 7:20-23).

These types of thoughts can lead to actions that lead us away from Jesus and down a path of personal destruction. So what will keep us from going down the wrong paths in life?

The apostle John has the answer:

This is the message we have heard from him and declare to you: God is light; in him there is no darkness at all. If we claim to have fellowship with him and yet walk in the darkness, we lie and do not live out the truth. But if we walk in the light, as he is in the light, we have fellowship with one another, and the blood of Jesus, his Son, purifies us from all sin.

If we claim to be without sin, we deceive

ourselves and the truth is not in us. If we confess our sins, he is faithful and just and will forgive us our sins and purify us from all unrighteousness. If we claim we have not sinned, we make him out to be a liar and his word is not in us.

My dear children, I write this to you so that you will not sin. But if anybody does sin, we have an advocate with the Father—Jesus Christ, the Righteous One. He is the atoning sacrifice for our sins, and not only for ours but also for the sins of the whole world. (1 John 1:5-10; 2:1,2)

That's true forgiveness—God's forgiveness.

ABOUT THE WRITER

Dr. Bruce Becker currently serves as the executive vice president for Time of Grace. He is also a respected and well-known church consultant, presenter, advisor, podcaster, and author. He has served as lead pastor of two congregations; as a member of several boards; and on many commissions, committees, and task forces. In 2012 he completed his professional doctorate in leadership and ministry management. Bruce and his wife, Linda, live in Jackson, Wisconsin. Find Dr. Becker's podcast, *Bible Threads With Dr. Bruce Becker*, at timeofgrace.org, Apple Podcasts, Spotify, and many other podcasting platforms.

ABOUT TIME OF GRACE

Time of Grace is an independent, donor-funded ministry that connects people to God's grace—his love, glory, and power—so they realize the temporary things of life don't satisfy. What brings satisfaction is knowing that because Jesus lived, died, and rose for all of us, we have access to the eternal God—right now and forever.

To discover more, please visit timeofgrace.org or call 800.661.3311.

HELP SHARE GOD'S MESSAGE OF GRACE!

Every gift you give helps Time of Grace reach people around the world with the good news of Jesus. Your generosity and prayer support take the gospel of grace to others through our ministry outreach and help them experience a satisfied life as they see God all around them.

Give today at timeofgrace.org/give or by calling 800.661.3311.

Thank you!